NELSON
A Cengage Company

 NEW HOUSE

understanding ECONOMICS

For NCEA Level One

EXTERNALS

Workbook RESOURCE

 Dan Rennie

Understanding Economics for NCEA Level One Workbook
5th Edition
Dan Rennie

Typeset by : *Book*NZ

Any URLs contained in this publication were checked for currency during the production process. Note, however, that the publisher cannot vouch for the ongoing currency of URLs.

Fourth edition published in 2013 by Cengage Learning Australia Pty Limited.

For product information and technology assistance,
in Australia call **1300 790 853**;
in New Zealand call **0800 449 725**

For permission to use material from this text or product, please email
aust.permissions@cengage.com

National Library of New Zealand Cataloguing-in-Publication Data
A catalogue record for this book is available from the National Library of New Zealand

ISBN 978 0 17 041597 2

Cengage Learning Australia
Level 7, 80 Dorcas Street
South Melbourne, Victoria Australia 3205

Cengage Learning New Zealand
Unit 4B Rosedale Office Park
331 Rosedale Road, Albany, North Shore 0632, NZ

For learning solutions, visit **cengage.co.nz**

Printed in China by 1010 Printing International Limited
7 8 9 10 25 24 23

Contents

A digital version of the *Teacher Resource*, which contains full answers to this workbook, is available via Vital Source for only $19.95 for 12 months.

For more information:

Email: nz.sales@cengage.com

Website: www.cengage.co.nz.

INTRODUCTION

Understanding Economics has been written for students who are studying Economics at Level One. It is a self-supporting workbook which provides the precise economic terms and questions to develop skills that students need to acquire.

Economics is an academic subject and students need to have economic ideas and language as set out in the prescription rather than rely on common knowledge or skills learned in other subjects. This book provides a multitude of activities, sometimes repeated, to encourage answering-precision and to discourage ambiguity.

Understanding Economics should not be used in isolation but rather in conjunction with text books, classroom notes and assignments. It can be used as either a source of homework or revision but it is mainly designed to provide teaching activities for the year's course.

My hope is that this workbook of activities for the complete course will save teachers time in writing, preparing and copying activities, while providing students with hours of successful work and study.

Dan Rennie

Notes to the student

1 Do all the exercises set by your teacher, making sure you mark these accurately and correct any errors. Do not be afraid of making mistakes. Learn from your mistakes.

2 Ask questions and ask for assistance to questions or topics that you have difficulty with; it is the only way to understand the topics of which you are unsure.

3 Model solutions to all exercises are in the Teacher's Guide.

4 Work is the key to success.

5 Good luck.

6 Digital answers to the questions can be obtained by contacting Cengage New Zealand, https://cengage.co.nz

      ISBN: 9780170415972

1 BASIC CONCEPTS
Central ideas

Needs and wants

Needs are things individuals must have in order to sustain life, such as food, clothes or shelter (warmth) and water.

Wants are those things individuals would like to have but are not necessary in order to survive, e.g., cell phones, TV, cars, overseas travel. Wants are unlimited as most things wear out and have to be replaced or because of greed. As soon as one level of satisfaction is achieved a new and higher level of satisfaction becomes the objective. Most individuals would like to have more or better things than they possess at the moment. For example, a fisherman may want a larger boat with the latest and best equipment available, something better than he currently has.

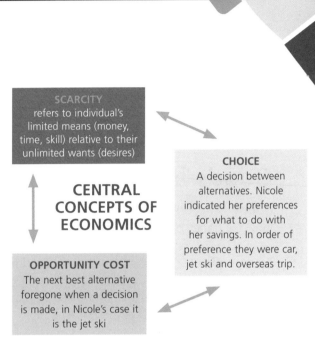

SCARCITY refers to individual's limited means (money, time, skill) relative to their unlimited wants (desires)

CENTRAL CONCEPTS OF ECONOMICS

CHOICE A decision between alternatives. Nicole indicated her preferences for what to do with her savings. In order of preference they were car, jet ski and overseas trip.

OPPORTUNITY COST The next best alternative foregone when a decision is made, in Nicole's case it is the jet ski

Usually individuals use their limited means (time, skills, knowledge, income and family) to first satisfy their needs then, if they have means left over, to satisfy their wants.

Basis of Economics

The central concept or basis of economics is how individuals and society try to satisfy **unlimited (infinite or insatiable) wants** using **scarce (finite or limited) resources**. There would be no economic problem if scarcity was eliminated.

Scarcity refers to the condition of limited means relative to an individual's or society's unlimited wants. The **limited means** that individuals have include money (income or wealth), skills or knowledge and time. All the world's population faces the problem of limited (finite or scarce) means, that of time, income and skill. Time is limited whether you are poor or wealthy. There are only 24 hours in a day and time spent on one activity can not be spent on another activity. Income (money) is a limited means for all people because money spent on one item can not be used to buy something else at the same time. There is a finite amount of money that people have or earn, meaning that even the rich can not have everything they want. Everyone has skills but no one person is good at everything, therefore the skills that an individual possesses are limited. Therefore, individuals and society can not have everything they want so must choose the option they want the most.

A **choice** is a decision between alternatives (options) that results from the condition of scarcity (limited means relative to unlimited wants). All individuals rich, poor or well off, firms and governments must make choices because they can not have everything. For example, Frank has to decide whether to go away for the weekend, or to go fishing with his father-in-law or stay at home and paint the front fence.

When a choice (decision) is made between alternatives there will be an opportunity cost. The **opportunity cost** refers to the next best alternative foregone of a decision, i.e., it is the second ranked alternative only missed out on. For example, if Frank decided to go fishing with his father-in-law and considered the least desirable alternative as painting the front fence, the opportunity cost is the weekend away. The opportunity cost is not the weekend away and painting the front fence because opportunity cost is singular, and so cannot apply to more than one item.

Producers and consumers

A **producer** is any person or organisation that uses resources (natural, human or capital goods) to create goods and services.

Consumers are individuals or households (a group of individuals) that consume (use) goods and services produced by producers (firms or businesses).

Goods and services

Goods (commodities) are objects (or items) that have a physical presence. Goods can be subdivided into free goods or economic goods.

Free goods are goods that are plentiful and have no cost, for example, wind and sunshine.

Economic goods are scarce and therefore have a cost. Economic goods can be subdivided into either consumer goods or capital (producer) goods.

Consumer goods are for consumption by individuals or households (a group of individuals) for their own private satisfaction (use), for example, DVDs, designer clothes.

Capital (producer) goods are man-made goods used in the production of other goods and services, for example, tools, machinery. The distinction between consumer goods and capital goods is not in the type of good but rather in the use to which the good is put; for example, a television used by a household is a consumer good but a television used by a firm as a security measure to prevent theft is a capital good.

Services are what someone does for you, such as the work of a mechanic or doctor.

       ISBN: 9780170415972

Terms & ideas

Limited means that consumers have	Income (money or wealth), time, skill and knowledge.
Needs	Things individuals must have in order to sustain life, e.g., food, clothes or shelter and water.
Wants	Things individuals would like to have but are not necessary in order to survive, e.g., cars, phones, designer clothes.
Scarcity	The economic term that describes the condition of limited resources relative to wants.
Choice	The economic term that relates to a decision between alternatives, example: a choice between going to a movie or renting a video.
Opportunity cost	The *next best alternative forgone* when a *decision is made*. It is the real cost of any decision and is the other good/service that could have been produced with the same resources.
People can't have everything they want	Because they have limited means (not enough money).
The relationship between limited means and the need to make decisions	We cannot have everything so we must make choices and every decision has an opportunity cost.
Choices ...	... are based on limited means (time, income, skill and knowledge).
Every choice means ...	... there will be an opportunity cost.
Goods	Objects with a physical presence, tangible items, examples: snowboard, fish.
Services	What someone does for you, example: giving ski lessons.

Student notes: Basic Concepts – Central ideas

ISBN: 9780170415972

QUESTIONS & TASKS

1 a Explain the difference between needs and wants.

_____

_____

_____

_____

_____

_____

_____

b Indicate if the following statements are true or false.

(i) Wants can also be needs because the first thing individuals want are the things they desire that are essential to survive, i.e., needs.   _____

(ii) A want is something an individual desires but that does not mean it is necessarily a need.   _____

(iii) An individual will always satisfy their needs before they satisfy their wants.   _____

c Explain your answer to **b (iii)** above with an example.

_____

_____

_____

d Francis lives at home with his parents and his younger sisters, Mary and Clare. His mother is a self-employed panelbeater. His father works in the business office part time and manages their home.

(i) Using the concept of limited means, explain why Francis' father only works part time when he could work full time in the family business.

_____

_____

(ii) Describe another way in which Francis' family may have limited means.

_____

_____

_____

2 Read the extracts and answer the questions that follow.

Hone receives $40 a week in pocket money as long as he completes the chores that he has to do. He cleans his uncle's workshop every day and earns $25 a week for this. He is saving some of his income for some diving gear and a snowboard he intends to buy. Hone would like to earn more money but finds he is too busy with his studies at school and cultural commitments.

a (i) If Hone buys a dive tank, what will be the opportunity cost of his decision?

_____

(ii) Explain why your answer to (i) is the opportunity cost.

_____

b Whanau (family) is one of the limited means used by Hone to satisfy his unlimited wants. List three other limited means Hone has.

(i) _____

(ii) _____

(iii) _____

Ryan is 16 and received $80 for his birthday but he can not decide what to buy. He has several options.
Option A: Buy CDs.
Option B: Repair his windsurfer.
Option C: Go rafting – the $80 would cover the price of the trip but not the train fare to the river, so he can only go if his mum can take him.

c All economic decisions have an opportunity cost. For Ryan, it was Option B. Define the economic idea of opportunity cost.

_____

_____

_____

d Describe two conflicts Ryan may face between his desire to go rafting and his limited means.

(i) _____

_____

(ii) _____

_____

e Identify why Ryan's limited means meant that he had to make a decision about how to spend his birthday money.

_____

_____

_____

_____

     ISBN: 9780170415972

3 Samantha attends school and works two nights a week at the local supermarket. She does assignments, shops, and trains for surf lifesaving three times a week. She would like to go away for a weekend with friends.

a Explain how time is a scarce resource for Samantha.

_____

_____

_____

_____

_____

_____

_____

b Describe what is meant by a **good** and a **service**. Provide a clear example of each.

Good _____

Good example _____

Service _____

Service example _____

c Connor has a part-time job working at the video store. This often means that he can't go out with his friends because he is working.

(i) If Connor takes a night off and goes with his friends to a party, what is the opportunity cost of his decision?

_____

(ii) Connor has limited means. Describe the concept of limited means.

_____

_____

_____

(iii) Explain how the idea of scarcity is linked to the consumers' need to make economic decisions.

_____

_____

_____

_____

_____

_____

_____

_____

4 Zac indicated his preferences for an overseas trip. In order of preference they were going to Bali, Fiji and Samoa.

Use the information to explain the concepts **opportunity cost**, **scarcity** and **choice**.

_____

_____

_____

_____

_____

_____

_____

_____

_____

_____

_____

_____

_____

_____

_____

_____

5 a Nathan has to choose between going rafting, snowboarding or fishing. He considers fishing as the most desirable activity and snowboarding as the least desirable. Explain the opportunity cost concept.

_____

_____

b Consumers must make decisions about what to do. Why can't they have everything they want?

_____

_____

c Describe the difference between a good and a service.

_____

_____

_____

_____

       ISBN: 9780170415972

6 a Who has unlimited means?

_____

_____

_____

_____

_____

_____

_____

_____

_____

_____

b Which of the following situations will have an opportunity cost?
  (i) A student decides to work full time.
  (ii) A family goes on an overseas trip rather than buying a second car.
  (iii) A free lunch at a brewery opening.

_____

_____

_____

_____

c Jason always has something to do, week nights are taken up doing homework, training for surf lifesaving (the most preferred option) and doing chores around home (the least preferred option). Despite his best efforts, he never manages to do all tasks in a single day. With specific reference to Jason, explain how limited means, choice and opportunity costs are linked.

_____

_____

_____

_____

_____

_____

_____

_____

_____

_____

_____

d Describe how an individual's means may be augmented by family (whanau).

_____

_____

_____

Review (exam) questions

Michael is twenty and works part time. He earns $100 per week. Michael is saving for a car and intends to buy either a DVD player or a computer. His sporting commitments, assignments and studies mean he is too busy to earn more. His birthday is coming up, and he asks his family to contribute towards a better computer instead of buying him presents.

1 Fully explain scarcity in relation to choices and opportunity cost for Michael. In your answer you should:

- Refer to the resource material and link the following: limited means, choice, opportunity cost.
- Explain how Michael's means have increased because of his family.

 ISBN: 9780170415972

Hamish has worked as a regional guard over the summer and saved $2000. He is thinking about spending this on either a phone, computer or a holiday with friends.

2 Explain how money is a limited means that affects Hamish's choice. In your answer you should discuss:
- scarcity
- opportunity cost.

Dani works weekends at the local takeaway shop. The rest of her time is spent on the following activities (in no particular order):

- training for surf lifesaving
- attending university
- spending time with her friends.

3 Explain how time is a limited resource for Dani. In your answer you should refer to the resource material above and discuss:

- scarcity
- choice
- opportunity cost.

_____

_____

_____

_____

_____

_____

_____

_____

_____

_____

_____

_____

_____

_____

_____

_____

_____

_____

_____

_____

_____

_____

_____

_____

    ISBN: 9780170415972

2 BASIC CONCEPTS
The choices we make

The influence of values on the choices we make

Consumers' choices (or decisions) will be influenced by the price of a good or service, the quality and features it may or may not have, their limited means (income, time, skill and knowledge), tastes and preferences, and their values. Individuals and households do not earn enough money or have the time to do everything they want, so must choose the cheapest option or the option that they want the most.

Values are key principles or core beliefs, or those things individuals consider most important. Values that individuals may hold include consideration of others, honesty, integrity and fair trading. **Fair trading** is doing what is right when dealing with others, that is, not cheating or deceiving them; for example, not selling eggs as organic or free range when they are not. Factors that may influence the different values that individuals may hold include religion, culture, gender, upbringing or family, age or experience and peer pressure.

A consumer's values will affect his or her behaviour, taste, preference and therefore demand for goods and services, for example, Jamie might not eat fish on Fridays because of her strict religious beliefs. When it comes to grocery shopping Ray buys products that are 'recyclable' or 'environmentally friendly', Sam always chooses the cheapest alternative available and Bill always buys the best quality, this shows that consumers bring different values to the decisions they make.

A conflict can arise over the values people hold and the choices individuals make. Jacob may consider it important that he is fit and healthy and is likely to want to spend time training at the gym but he also considers it important to be financially secure so will want to spend time at work earning an income. To resolve this conflict, Jacob could decide to attend the gym early in the morning and then go to work. In this way, he can earn an income for financial security as well as keeping fit and healthy.

Key terms and ideas

Values	Core beliefs or key principles that we consider most important. People bring different values to economic decision-making.	
Examples of values people might hold	• Honesty • Integrity	• Consideration of others • Fair trading
Fair trading	Doing what is right and just when dealing with others (not cheating or deceiving others); for example not turning back the speedo on a car, not selling fish as 'fresh' when it isn't.	
Factors that influence values people hold	• Upbringing • Culture or cultural beliefs • Gender	• Peer pressure • Media • Age/experience • Religion or religious beliefs
Example of values that affect decisions consumers make	A person doesn't steal because of his or her upbringing which values honesty.	

Student notes: Basics concepts – The choices we make

 ISBN: 9780170415972

QUESTIONS & TASKS

1 Jamie works at the local pizza shop after school. Her friends go swimming at the beach.

   a (i) If Jamie decides to go swimming, what is the opportunity cost of going with her friends?

       _____

     (ii) Why is this the opportunity cost?

       _____

       _____

   b With reference to the information in the extract, explain the concept of choice.

       _____

       _____

       _____

   c Jamie has limited means. Describe the concept of limited means.

       _____

Jamie's sister Jessie has saved up money to buy a car and has yet to make a decision on which car to buy. Her 20th birthday is coming up and she has asked her extended family not to buy her a present but contribute towards the car.

   d How have Jessie's means increased because of her extended family?

       _____

       _____

       _____

2 a Explain what is meant by the term 'values'.

       _____

       _____

       _____

   b List several factors that may determine the values that people hold.

       _____

       _____

       _____

   c List examples of values that people may hold.

       _____

       _____

       _____

3 Read the resource and answer the questions that follow.

Caitlin has just finished High School and is looking forward to the summer break. She intends to play touch with her friends and work picking strawberries to save money for her course fees. Caitlin is a consumer of books, DVDs and Playstation games, going to the movies and eating takeaways.

a Describe what is meant by a consumer.

_____

_____

_____

_____

b Explain what is meant by fair trading. Include an example in your answer.

_____

_____

_____

_____

_____

Consideration of others is a value Caitlin holds.

c Explain how this value may influence how Caitlin spends her income.

_____

_____

_____

_____

d Identify the value in the table. Select from: Integrity, Travel/adventure, Fair trading/Honesty, Consideration of others, Financial security.

Situation	Value
(i) Marty tells the buyer of his car that it will not pass a warrant because of the rust.	
(ii) An individual goes to church and holds fast to a set of moral principles for how they live their life.	
(iii) Greg, who donates money to charity.	
(iv) Bill, who decides to go on a holiday overseas.	
(v) Mel, who puts money aside in a bank account.	

       ISBN: 9780170415972

4 Read the resource material and answer the questions that follow.

Each week Tony and Margaret go to church and assist in the local charity shop.

a **(i)** Identify the value that Tony and Margaret hold.

_____

_____

(ii) Explain why they might hold this value.

_____

_____

_____

b Explain a link between a value you may hold and an economic decision you make.

A belief in keeping fit and healthy   A belief in being a positive role model   (Circle one)

A belief in the importance of education   A belief in treating others fairly

Explanation: _____

_____

_____

_____

_____

_____

_____

_____

_____

_____

c **(i)** List the limited means you have.

_____

_____

_____

Tony and Margaret have two brothers-in-law, one is a builder and the other is an electrician.

(ii) How have Tony and Margaret's means increased because of their extended whanau?

_____

_____

_____

_____

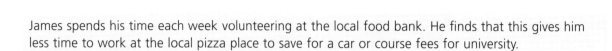

James spends his time each week volunteering at the local food bank. He finds that this gives him less time to work at the local pizza place to save for a car or course fees for university.

5 Discuss how James's values influence his spending decisions. In your answer you should:
- explain what is meant by 'values'
- describe a value James demonstrates when volunteering at the local food bank
- describe a value James demonstrates when choosing to go to university
- explain how James's values could conflict, and a compromise he could make to resolve this conflict.

6 a Christian believes it is important to travel and live a healthy lifestyle. Explain how his values may influence how he spends his money. In your answer discuss any conflict that may arise out of his decision and a compromise that he could use to satisfy both his values.

_____

_____

_____

_____

_____

_____

_____

_____

_____

_____

_____

b Emma works part-time at the local pizza place during the week. She divides the rest of her time between studying, going to the gym and visiting her family and friends. What activity will Emma most likely do if she values (i) financial security, (ii) education, (iii) her health?

_____

_____

_____

_____

c In making a decision, a consumer must consider their values (which could include consideration of others and the importance of keeping fit and healthy). Fully explain how values influence the economic decision a consumer may make. In your answer: (i) define what is meant by a consumer and values, (ii) describe why consumers may hold different values, and (iii) explain how values held by consumers will influence the decisions they make.

_____

_____

_____

_____

_____

_____

_____

_____

_____

_____

Review (exam) questions

Ray lives in a flat. He works part time at the local pool. The main activities he chooses to spend his time on are: working at a local gym (least preferred option), attending university (main priority) and spending time reading a book.

1 Explain how scarcity and values affect consumer choice. Explain how time is a limited resource for Ray. In your answer you should refer to the resource material above and discuss:
- scarcity
- choice
- opportunity cost.

Fully explain the way values might influence how Ray chooses to spend his time. In your answer you should refer to the main activities on the previous page that Ray chooses to spend his time on, and discuss:

- the most likely activity Ray will spend his time doing if he values his education
- the most likely activity Ray will spend his time doing if he values financial stability
- conflict that might arise over the two decisions above
- one way in which Ray may resolve this conflict.

_____

_____

_____

_____

_____

_____

_____

_____

_____

_____

_____

_____

_____

_____

_____

_____

_____

_____

_____

_____

_____

_____

_____

_____

_____

_____

_____

_____

_____

_____

George boards with his uncle and his family. He works weekends at the video store. The following are the main activities he chooses to spend his time on: saving for course fees for university, travel around Australia and surf, working at the beach as a regional guard over the summer and going to the gym. George has saved $3000 and is pondering his options.

2 Fully explain how money is a limited resource and affects George's decision. In your answer you should refer to the resource material above and discuss:
- scarcity
- choice
- opportunity cost.

   ISBN: 9780170415972

Explain the way values might influence how George chooses to spend his time. Refer to the main activities that he chooses to spend his time on, and discuss:

- the most likely activity George will spend his time doing if he values adventure
- the most likely activity George will spend his time doing if he values his health
- conflict that might arise over the two decisions above and a way in which George may resolve this conflict.

_____

_____

_____

_____

_____

_____

_____

_____

_____

_____

_____

_____

_____

_____

_____

_____

_____

_____

_____

_____

_____

_____

_____

_____

_____

_____

3 DEMAND
Basic concepts

Demand, demand schedules and the law of demand

Wants are the unlimited or infinite desires that consumers have for goods or services that are not backed by the ability to pay.

Demand is the quantity of a good or service an individual is willing and able to buy at various prices. A demand is a desire backed by the ability to pay and therefore limited or finite. Effective demand is a want (desire) backed by the ability to pay.

Consumer (individual) demand is the amount of a good or service that one individual is willing and able to buy at various prices.

Title that includes the name of the consumer, what is demanded and in what time period

The heading of Price in the left-hand column with units

A heading of Quantity demanded in the right-hand column with units

Pete's demand schedule for organic chicken each month	
Price $ per kg	Quantity Demanded Kgs
5	15
10	10
15	5

Figures in either ascending or descending order accurately reflecting information from a graph or resource material

A **demand schedule** is a table of figures that relates the price to the quantity demanded. The information in a demand schedule assumes that all other factors that may influence demand are held constant. The Latin term ceteris paribus describes this assumption of holding all other factors unchanged. This allows us to see clearly the relationship between price and quantity demanded. To construct or draw up a demand schedule, certain conventions (rules) are followed. These are shown above.

The **law of demand** states that as the price of a good or service decreases, the quantity demanded increases, ceteris paribus. Or, as the price of a good or service increases, the quantity demanded decreases, ceteris paribus. Consumers will buy more at a lower price because they can afford more with their limited income or they are more willing and able to buy the good or service. Also, as the price of a good or service falls it will be relatively cheaper than a substitute.

Drawing a demand curve

A **demand curve** shows the information from a demand schedule or resource material graphically. When drawing a demand curve certain conventions or rules that should be followed are listed beside Pete's demand curve for organic chicken. Note that the price is on the Y (vertical) axis and the quantity demanded is on the X (horizontal) axis.

The shape of the demand curve (which slopes downwards to the right) follows the law of demand. A demand curve shows that price and quantity have an inverse relationship, i.e that price and quantity demanded are negatively related.

       ISBN: 9780170415972

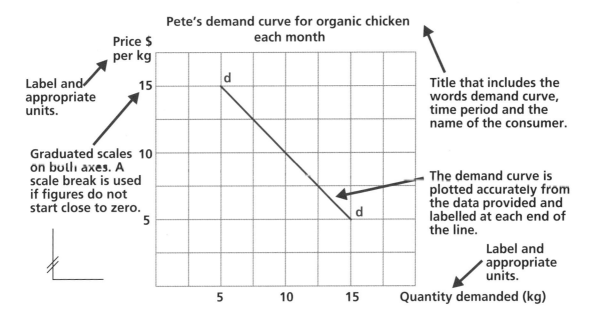

Label and appropriate units.

Graduated scales on both axes. A scale break is used if figures do not start close to zero.

Title that includes the words demand curve, time period and the name of the consumer.

The demand curve is plotted accurately from the data provided and labelled at each end of the line.

Label and appropriate units.

The demand curve slopes downwards from left to right for a normal good (a normal luxury or a normal necessity) because when the price of a good falls a consumer's real income rises and the good becomes relatively more affordable, a consumer will be willing and able to buy more of the product with their limited income and less of a relatively more expensive substitute. A substitute is a good or service that can satisfy similar needs for a consumer and can therefore be used to replace one another, for example, chicken or beef used in a curry.

A movement along a demand curve

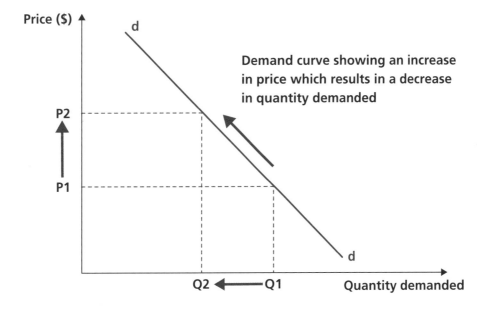

Demand curve showing an increase in price which results in a decrease in quantity demanded

To show a price change (movement along) a demand curve, label the original price P or P1 and the original quantity demanded Q or Q1. The new price is labelled P' or P2 and the new quantity demanded is labelled Q' or Q2. Direction arrows are used to show the direction of the change in price and quantity demanded, from the original position to the new position. Dotted lines are used to show the appropriate points on the demand curve to the price and quantity axes.

An increase in price causes a decrease in quantity demanded, illustrated by a movement up the demand curve to the left. A decrease in price causes an increase in quantity demanded, illustrated by a movement down the demand curve to the right.

Key terms and ideas

Ceteris paribus	All other factors (not price) being equal/held constant.
Law of demand	A fall in the price of a good or service will lead to an increase in quantity demanded, ceteris paribus (or vice versa).
Individual demand (or consumer demand)	The amount of a good or service one individual is willing and able to buy at various prices. If a price decreases, consumers are more willing and able to buy more.
Show a price (movement) change on a demand curve. **You must read the question and show the appropriate change asked for. The change in price and quantity demanded are in opposite directions so the graph shows a price decrease resulting in an increase in quantity demanded.**	P shows the original price asked for and P′ the new price (the arrow drawn on the vertical axis shows the direction of the price change, either an increase or decrease). The original price (P) relates to a specific original quantity demanded which is labelled Q, and Q′ will represent the new quantity demanded from the new price (P′). The arrow will show the direction of the change.
Demand schedule questions will ask you to (i) name the table or (ii) construct a schedule from a given graph or from resource material	Correct units — Write quantity demanded – not just quantity — Correct units — Numbers in correct order and accurately reflecting information from graph or resource material **Demand schedule for ...** Price $ per kg / Quantity demanded kg (00) 4 / 10 8 / 7 12 / 3
Why consumers buy more at lower prices (or when income increases)	If price decreases, consumers can now afford to buy more or they are more willing and able to buy the goods or services.
Value of original consumer spending	Price multiplied by quantity demanded (P x Q).
Value of new spending	New price multiplied by new quantity demanded (P′ x Q′).

Student notes: Demand – Basic concepts

QUESTIONS & TASKS

1 **a** Draw up the demand curve of the schedule below.

Annabelle's demand schedule for new release DVDs each month	
Price ($)	Quantity Demanded
4	11
5	9
6	7
7	5
8	3
9	1

b **(i)** On your graph, show the effect of the price of DVDs increasing from $5 to $8. Fully label your changes.

(ii) Identify the change in the number of DVDs that Annabelle will buy and the change in the value of her spending.

_____

_____

_____

_____

_____

(iii) Explain, with reasons, why the quantity of DVDs demanded by Annabelle changes when the price of DVDs increases.

_____

_____

_____

_____

(iv) Explain a flow-on effect this change will have for Annabelle.

_____

_____

_____

_____

_____

       ISBN: 9780170415972

2 a Use the information below to help answer the questions that follow. Use the grid below to draw the demand curve to show Basil's demand for chocolate bars in July.

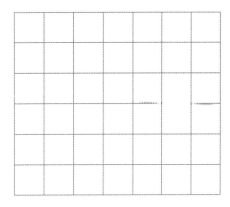

JULY

At a price of $2.00 Basil was prepared to purchase five chocolate bars. At $2.50 he would be willing to purchase three chocolate bars while at $3.00 two would be purchased. Basil would buy one chocolate bar if the price was $4.00.

b What does 'ceteris paribus' mean? _____

3 a For the resource material given in the box, draw up an appropriate demand schedule and then draw the appropriate demand curve for Dave's demand each month.

Dave buys live crayfish at the side of the road. If the price is $30, 11 are bought, while only three are bought if the price is $90.

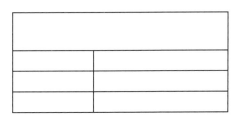

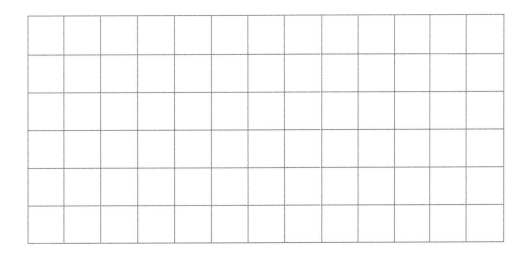

b (i) Show the quantity Dave would demand at a current price of $60.
(ii) Show the effect of a 25% decrease in price. Fully label your graph.
(iii) State the value of spending by Dave at the original price and the new price.

_____

_____

4 a Draw up the graph for the schedule below.

Simon's demand schedule for pies for lunch each month	
Price ($)	Quantity demanded
1	40
2	24
3	16

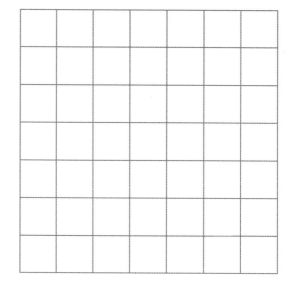

b (i) Show a price change from $2.50 to $1.00. Fully label your changes.

(ii) State the law of demand, then explain how the demand curve illustrates the law of demand using data from **(i)** above.

_____

_____

_____

_____

_____

(iii) Give reasons for the change in the number of pies that Simon will consume.

_____

_____

_____

_____

_____

(iv) Explain a flow-on effect this price change may have for Simon.

_____

_____

_____

_____

_____

_____

_____

5 Jacob was prepared to purchase one secondhand book at a price of $10 each month; he is willing to buy 15 at $2. Also, at $4 seven are sold and three are sold at $6.

a Complete the schedule below and then graph the information.

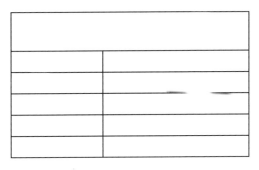

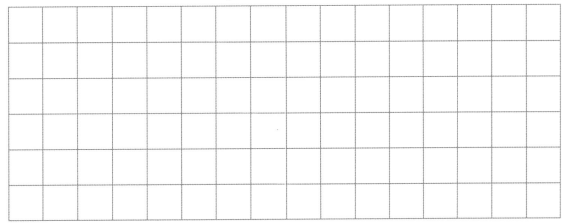

b Use the information in the demand schedule and demand curve to answer the following questions.

(i) How many secondhand books were sold at $5? _____

(ii) At what price were 2 secondhand books sold? _____

c Explain if it is possible to predict how many secondhand books would be sold at $1.00 using the information in the demand schedule above.

_____

_____

_____

d Indicate on the demand curve you drew the effect of a price increase of 100% from an original price of $4.

e What is demand?

_____

_____

_____

_____

6 Jim indicates in a survey on chewing gum that at $0.85 he would buy 24 packets each month and at $1.05 he would demand six. Also at $1.00 he would buy seven and 14 at $0.90.

a Draw a demand curve for this information.

Jim's demand curve for chewing gum each month

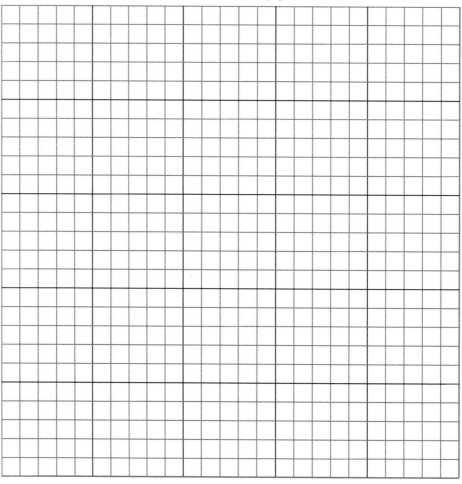

b Use the demand curve you drew above to calculate demand at $0.95. _____

c Show on your graph the effect of a change in price from $0.90 to $1.05.

d Describe the effect of a change in price from $0.90 to $1.05.

_____

_____

e What does 'ceteris paribus' mean?

_____

_____

f The Law of Demand states that when price decreases, quantity demanded increases, ceteris paribus. Use an example to explain how this may not always be true.

_____

_____

_____

       ISBN: 9780170415972

7   Anton decides to sell wind wands at the local market. He can make 12 each week. Over the next few weeks he experiments with the price. Only five sell when the price is $60 per wind wand, but his whole week's supply is purchased if the price is $18.

a   Use the above data and label a demand curve for Anton's wind wands.

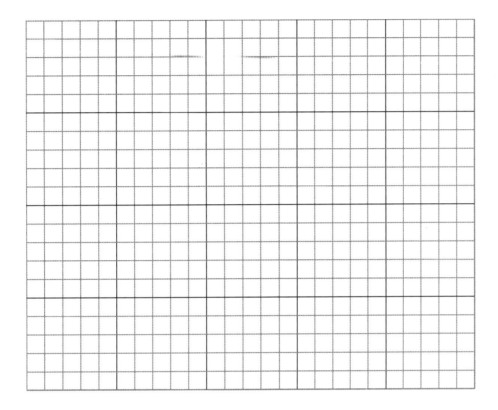

b   Use the demand curve you drew above to calculate the number of wind wands Anton would sell at $36.

_____

c   Why do Anton's customers buy more as the price falls?

_____

_____

d   Explain how a want is different from a demand.

_____

_____

e   State the price per wind wand if the quantity demanded was 7.   _____

f   State the value of spending by a consumer at:

   (i) $60 _____

   (ii) $30 _____

   (iii) $18 _____

8 a Use the information in the demand curve below to draw a **demand schedule** for bottles of water.

Demand curve for 600ml bottles of water per year

b Use the information in the demand schedule to answer the following questions.

(i) How many bottles were sold at $2.40? _____

(ii) At what price were 250 bottles sold? _____

(iii) How many bottles would have been sold at $2.10? _____

c Explain if it is possible to predict how many bottles would be sold in a year at $3.00 by using the information in the demand schedule above.

_____

_____

d Define consumer demand.

_____

_____

e Describe what a demand schedule illustrates.

_____

_____

_____

_____

_____

_____

f Describe what is meant by a consumer.

_____

_____

_____

    ISBN: 9780170415972

9 When a local pizza store started offering specials, so did the local fish and chip shop.

a (i) What is the name for the table below?

_____

(ii) The table shows that price and quantity demanded have an inverse relationship. State the economic term for this relationship.

_____

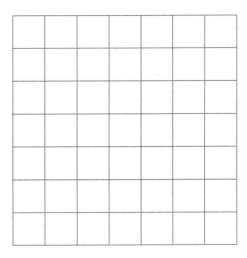

Jan's demand table for pieces of fish each month	
Price ($)	Quantity (per month)
2.00	12
3.00	6
6.00	2

b Use the information in the demand schedule above to draw Jan's demand curve for pieces of fish per month. Fully label your graph.

c How many pieces of fish would Jan buy at $3.00?

_____

d (i) On the graph, illustrate a price decrease from $6.00 to $3.00.

(ii) Explain the effect on quantity demanded.

_____

_____

(iii) If the price decreased from $6.00 to $3.00, explain the effect on Jan's spending on fish.

_____

_____

10 Jeremy's demand for international rocks concerts each year was that at $50 he would go to 14 concerts. If the price rose to $100 he would go to 9, and at $200 just 4. At a price of $300, quantity demanded would be just 2.

    a Draw Jeremy's yearly demand curve for international rock concerts on the grid below.

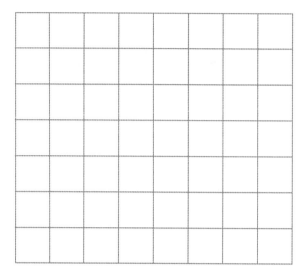

    b Show the effect of a change in price from $300 to $100. Label this answer fully.

    c Discuss the law of demand by referring to Jeremy's demand for international rock concerts. In your answer:
- Describe the law of demand by referring to the relevant data from question **b**.
- Explain, with reasons, why the quantity of international rock concerts demanded by Jeremy changes when the price falls.
- Explain several flow-on effects for Jeremy of the change in the number of concerts he attends.

         ISBN: 9780170415972

11 a Use the information in the demand curve below to draw a **demand schedule** in the space provided.

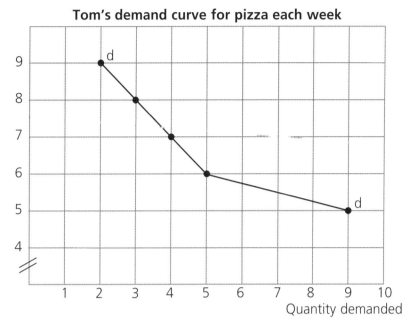

Tom's demand curve for pizza each week

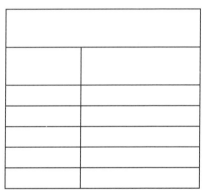

b On the graph above, show the effect of the price of pizza decreasing 25% from an original price of $8.

c Fully explain the change in the amount of pizza Tom will consume as the price decreases 25% from $8.

_____

_____

_____

_____

_____

d Explain a flow-on effect this price change will have for Tom.

_____

_____

_____

_____

_____

Review (exam) questions

Price and quantity demanded have an inverse relationship.

1 Explain the relationship between price and quantity demanded. In your answer you should:
- draw a demand curve using the schedule opposite and the grid provided
- describe what is meant by a consumer and consumer demand
- show a price increase from $15 per book of 100% and give reasons for the change in the number of paperback books purchased
- fully explain several flow-on effects this price change may have on Julian.

Julian's demand schedule for new release paperback books each year	
Price ($)	Quantity Demanded
5	13
10	11
15	9
20	8
25	7
30	6

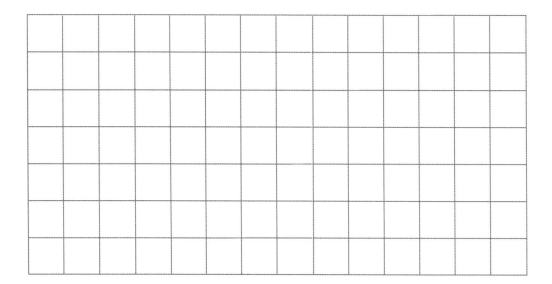

_____

_____

_____

_____

_____

_____

_____

_____

_____

_____

_____

As part of what he does during each month, Steve usually goes go-karting to catch up with and talk to his mates. At $30 per session he will do 10 sessions. When the price doubles he will go 6 times. At $100 he attends twice, and half this if the price is $120.

2 Fully explain the law of demand in the context of Steve's demand. In your answer you should:
- draw a demand curve using the information above. Show the effect of the price of go-karting sessions changing from $30 to $80
- with reference to the law of demand, discuss the changes in the number of go-karting sessions Steve may attend as the price of each session rises from $30 to $80
- explain flow-on effects this price change may have on Steve.

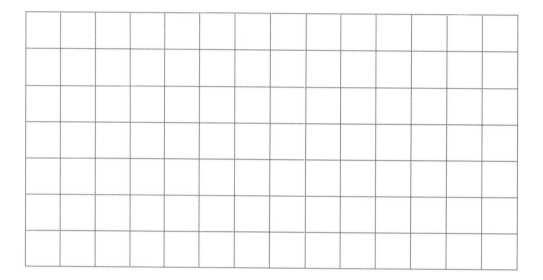

_____
_____
_____
_____
_____
_____
_____
_____
_____
_____
_____
_____
_____

     ISBN: 9780170415972

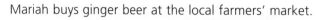

Mariah buys ginger beer at the local farmers' market.

Mariah's weekly demand schedule for ginger beer	
Price ($)	Quantity demanded (bottles)
7	1
5	5
4	8
3	13

3 Using the axes provided below, draw Mariah's weekly demand curve for ginger beer. Fully label your graph. On your graph show the effect of a price decrease from $6 to $4 per bottle for Mariah's ginger beer. Fully label the changes. In your answer you should:

- describe the law of demand, by referring to relevant data from your graph
- fully explain the effect of the price decrease, by referring to relevant data
- fully explain what Mariah might do if the price for her ginger beer increases above $8 a bottle.

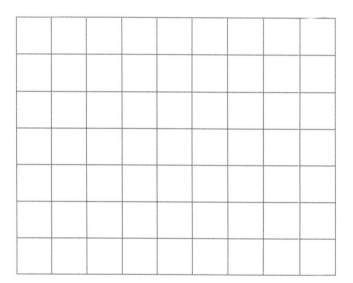

_____

_____

_____

_____

_____

_____

_____

_____

_____

_____

4 DEMAND
Conditions/shifts

Conditions of demand

A change in the **price** of a good or service causes a **movement along** an existing demand curve and a **change in quantity demanded**. A change in **conditions or determinants of demand** causes a demand curve to **shift** to an entirely new position, either inward (to the left) or outward (to the right) and a **change in demand**. Conditions or determinants of demand include tastes or fashion, incomes, direct tax, the price of a complement, the price of a substitute, advertising and events.

Disposable income is income after direct (income) taxes are paid and any transfers received. When direct (income) tax rates are cut or transfers increase then disposable incomes rise. As disposable incomes increase consumers can afford more and there will be an outward (to the right) shift of the demand curve for a good or service.

Substitutes are goods and services that can be used in place of each other, for example, staying at a backpackers or a hotel for accommodation, olive oil or vegetable oil used for cooking, chicken or beef used in a curry. A substitute is a good or service that can satisfy similar needs for a consumer and can therefore be used to replace one another. When the price of a substitute increases there will be a decrease in quantity demanded and the alternative product will see an increase in demand, because it is now relatively cheaper and consumers will buy more of it.

Complements are goods and services that are used together. With complementary goods the use of one good involves the use of another interrelated good or service. Examples of complements include cars and petrol, pen and paper, golf membership and golf clubs. When the price of a complement decreases there will be an increase in quantity demanded and the product used in conjunction with the complement will see an increase in demand because consumers will buy more of it to go with the product it is used in conjunction with. For example, demand for hired skis will increase if the price of a complement falls, such as a ski lift pass that allows individuals access to use a ski field. More skis will be hired because individuals who have purchased a ski lift pass will need skis to use on the ski slopes.

Shifts of the demand curve

When we **relax the assumption ceteris paribus the demand curve will shift** to an entirely new position or a new demand schedule will be drawn up. **At each and every price there is a new quantity demanded.**

Jane's demand schedule for bottled water in January and March		
Price $	Quantity demanded January (bottles)	Quantity demanded March (bottles)
1.00	3	6
2.00	2	5
3.00	1	4

Note at each and every price there is an increase in quantity demanded which we term an increase in demand

A shift of the demand curve to the **right (outward)** is termed an **increase in demand**, this means that at each and every price there is an increase in quantity demanded. A shift of the demand curve to the **left (inward)** is termed a **decrease in demand**, this means that at each and every price there is a decrease in quantity demanded.

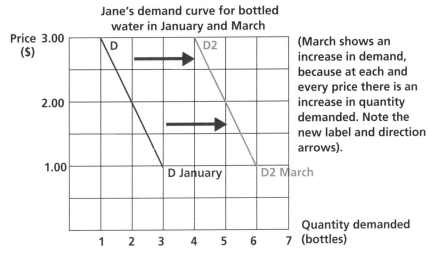

Jane's demand curve for bottled water in January and March

(March shows an increase in demand, because at each and every price there is an increase in quantity demanded. Note the new label and direction arrows).

The new demand curve is drawn parallel to the original demand curve and labelled D' or D2. Arrows are used to show the direction of the shift of the curve. The change in demand can be illustrated in a demand schedule or demand curve as shown.

The **conditions or determinants of demand** that will cause the demand curve to shift include tastes (fashion), incomes, price of a complement, price of a substitute, advertising and events.

Reasons for shifts of the demand curve

The reasons for the demand curve shifting **outward to the right (an increase in demand)** for bottled water could be:

- An **increase in consumers' disposable income**. Disposable income is income after direct (income) taxes are paid and any transfers received. When direct (income) tax rates are cut or transfers increase then disposable incomes rise. As disposable incomes increase consumers can afford more and there will be an outward (to the right) shift of the demand curve for bottled water (from D to D2) . This represents that at each and every price there is an increase in quantity demanded (termed an increase in demand).
- An **increase in the price of a substitute**. When the price of bottled fruit juice (a substitute for bottled water) increases there will be a decrease in quantity demanded for bottled fruit juice but there will be an increase in demand (outward shift of the demand curve) for bottled water because bottled water is **relatively cheaper**.
- A **decrease in the price of a complement**. A sporting event and bottled water could be considered to be complements because they are products that are used in conjunction with each other. As the price of a sporting event decreases the quantity demanded increases, ceteris paribus, because the sporting event is more affordable. Consumers will buy more bottled water to drink as they compete.
- A change in the size of a country's **population** or a change in its composition (age or gender) impacts on demand. An **increase in population** due to a net migration gain increases the number of consumers in the market, **more buyers** in the market can translate to an increase in demand for bottled water.

Events can cause demand to increase (or decrease). An earthquake can raise concerns about water quality supplied by a local council or authority since water pipes can break or raw sewage or wastewater may contaminate the water table. This will increase demand for bottled water because consumers will want to drink bottled water because they know it is safe to consume and will not endanger their health. An impending storm may cause consumers to stock up on essential supplies such as bottled water, which will increase demand.

An **advertising** campaign that **raises consumer awareness** of the health benefits of drinking bottled water or convinces individuals that bottled water tastes better, is cleaner and is the most convenient way to drink water is likely to increase demand.

Consumer **preferences or tastes** will impact on demand. If there is a shift in consumer **habits or taste toward** individuals drinking bottled water, then demand for bottled water will increase.

Key terms and ideas

What will cause the demand curve to shift?	Change in conditions of demand (determinants) • income • taste/fashion • income (direct) taxes • price of substitute • advertising • price of complement
Complements	Products that go or are used together, for example, cars and petrol, hot dogs and tomato sauce. A price increase in one causes demand for the other product to decrease.
Substitutes	Products that can be used in place of something else, for example, butter in place of margarine, coffee in place of tea, beef in place of lamb. A price increase for one product causes demand for the other product to increase.
Causes of a shift of the demand curve to the right (i.e., an increase in demand)	• increased disposable incomes • decreased income (direct) tax • increased advertising for product • price of a complement falls • price of a substitute increases • product is more in fashion
Causes of a shift of the demand curve to the left (i.e., a decrease in demand):	• decreased disposable incomes • increased income (direct) tax • price of a complement rises • price of a substitute decreases • product is out of fashion

  ISBN: 9780170415972

Student notes: Demand – Conditions/shifts

ISBN: 9780170415972

QUESTIONS & TASKS

1 a Complete the table below.

Product	Possible complement	Possible substitute
Tennis membership		
10 speed bike		
Snowboard		
Motorcar		
DVD player		

b Complete the sketch graph below to illustrate an **increase in quantity demanded**. Fully label your graph and use arrows to illustrate the change.

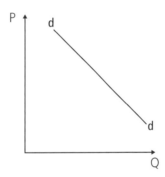

c Complete the sketch graph below to illustrate an **increase in demand**. Fully label your graph and use arrows to illustrate the change.

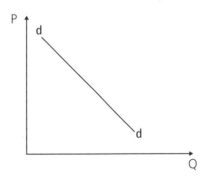

d Explain the difference between an **increase in quantity demanded** and an **increase in demand**.

_____

_____

_____

_____

_____

2 a Explain the difference between a substitute and a complement. Use examples.

_____

_____

_____

_____

b List two causes (other than changing the price of substitutes for DVDs) that could shift the demand curve for DVDs to the right, i.e., increase the demand for DVDs. For each cause, give the reason to explain why the demand curve will shift to the right.

Cause 1: _____

Reason: _____

_____

_____

Cause 2: _____

Reason: _____

_____

_____

c What is demand?

_____

_____

d Explain why an increase in price does **not** result in a decrease in demand.

_____

_____

_____

e Place the following pairs of products listed in the box into the correct column in the table below.

Cars and WOF, tea and coffee, pork and lamb, vegemite and marmite, bread and butter, strawberries and cream, DVDs and videos, apples and oranges

Substitutes	Complements

3 a (i) On **Graph 1**, below, sketch the likely impact of a **fall** in the **price** of cell phone calls on Brooke's demand for cell phone calls. Use appropriate lines, labels and arrows.

Brooke's demand for cell phone calls

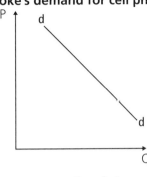

Graph 1

(ii) Describe the change you have shown on **Graph 1**.

_____

_____

_____

(iii) Explain the change you have shown in **Graph 1**.

_____

_____

_____

_____

_____

b (i) On **Graph 2**, below, sketch the likely impact of a fall in the price of cell phone calls on Brooke's demand for texting. Use appropriate lines, labels and arrows.

Brooke's demand for texting

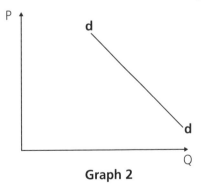

Graph 2

(ii) Describe the change you have shown on **Graph 2**.

_____

(iii) Explain the change you have shown in **Graph 2**.

_____

_____

_____

_____

4 Movement shifts description. Write ONE of the following for each situation given below.

- increase in demand
- decrease in demand
- increase in quantity demanded
- decrease in quantity demanded

SITUATION (for cans of Frank's cola)	DESCRIPTION (for cans of Frank's cola)
a shift of the curve to the right	
b a price decrease for cans of Frank's cola	
c a price increase for cans of Frank's cola	
d a shift to the left	
e an increase in people's disposable income	
f a decrease in income tax rates	
g increased advertising for cans of Frank's cola	
h **Cans of Frank's cola**	
i the price of a can of a competitor's cola falls by 50%	
j	
k drinking Frank's cola is a craze	
l the price of a can of a competitor's cola increases by 25%	

5 Demand for Air Gordon basketball shoes. Tick (✔) the appropriate boxes.

Demand for Air Gordons	Tick (✔) one of these		Tick (✔) only ONE of these			
	Movement along demand curve	Shift of demand curve	Increase in quantity demanded	Decrease in quantity demanded	Increase in demand	Decrease in demand
a Air Gordons fall in price						
b Increased advertising on TV and radio for Air Gordons						
c The NBA endorses Air Gordon shoes						
d It is fashionable to wear Air Gordons						
e A rival shoe decreases its price (on Air Gordons)						
f A complement used with Air Gordons falls in price						
g The price of Air Gordons rises						
h Air Gordons cause major injuries to all players in all grades						
i A shift of the curve right						
j A competitor's shoe has a very successful advertising/promotion						

6 a What is the ONLY cause of a movement along a demand curve?

_____

b Match the graph to the situation given in the table below.

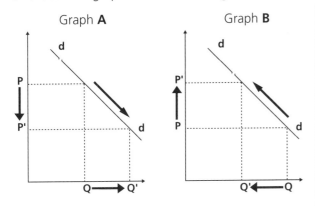

Graph **A**   Graph **B**

SITUATION	GRAPH A or B or NEITHER
(i) price decrease for a product	
(ii) increase in quantity demanded	
(iii) decrease in quantity demanded	
(iv) a price increase for a product	
(v) an increase in demand	
(vi) a change in conditions of demand	
(vii) an increase in people's income	
(viii) increased advertising	

c Match the graph to the situation given in the table.

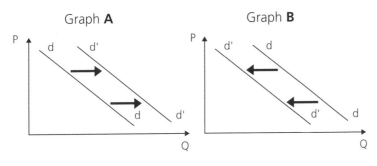

Graph **A**   Graph **B**

SITUATION	GRAPH A or B or NEITHER
(i) a shift right	
(ii) an increase in demand	
(iii) an increase in quantity demanded	
(iv) a shift left	
(v) a decrease in demand	
(vi) a decrease in quantity demanded	
(vii) increase in people's incomes	
(viii) increased advertising	

d Explain what is the cause of a 'shift' of a demand curve.

_____

_____

e Match each graph with the situation below.

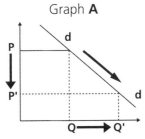 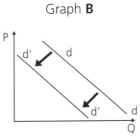 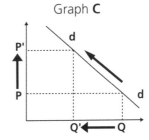 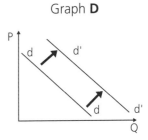

Graph **A**   Graph **B**   Graph **C**   Graph **D**

SITUATION FOR TROPICAL JUICES	GRAPH	SITUATION FOR TROPICAL JUICES	GRAPH
(i) Price fall of juices		**(vii)** Increased advertising for juices	
(ii) A decrease in demand		**(viii)** An increase in demand	
(iii) A decrease in quantity demanded		**(ix)** A shift of the demand curve to the left	
(iv) A shift of the demand curve to the right		**(x)** The price of an ice-block falls to 30 cents	
(v) A long hot summer		**(xi)** The price of tropical juices falls to 40 cents	
(vi) More pupils find jobs after school			

7 Treena enjoys going to the movies. At \$4 per ticket she would go to 10 movies per month, but if the price doubled she would only go to 4 movies per month. She would see 2 movies at a price of \$12 per ticket but would see 7 movies if the price was \$6 per ticket.

a Use the above information to complete Treena's demand curve for movies per month on the grid below.

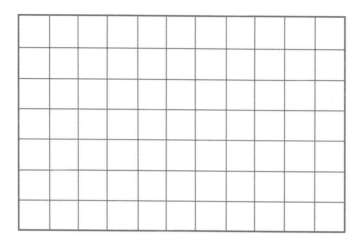

b Suggest a suitable reason why each of the following situations could occur.

(i) At \$14 per movie, Treena chooses not to see any movies. _____

_____

(ii) At \$6 per movie, Treena chooses to see five movies. _____

_____

_____

_____

(iii) At \$12 per movie, Treena chooses to see three movies. _____

_____

_____

_____

(iv) Treena chooses to see four movies instead of two movies. Assume no change to her demand curve.

_____

c (i) On your graph above show the effect of a 50% fall in Treena's demand for movies. Fully label the changes you make.

(ii) Explain a flow-on effect of this change for Treena.

_____

_____

_____

_____

    ISBN: 9780170415972

8 A local rock band 'Nothing at All' is told the following could happen to its demand for various situations:

- increase in demand
- decrease in demand
- increase in quantity demanded
- decrease in quantity demanded

Match ONE only of the above for each situation below.

Situation	Description
Example: price to see 'Nothing at All' increases	decrease in quantity demanded
a a shift to the right	
b a shift to the left	
c tickets to see the band fall in price (i.e. 'Nothing at All' prices fall)	
d 'Nothing at All' Demand Curve	
e increased advertising for 'Nothing at All'	
f students' income increases with the decrease in income tax	
g 'Nothing at All' Demand Curve	
h 'Nothing at All' is the band of the moment	
i A rival band lowers its ticket price	
j 'Nothing at All' Demand Curve	

9 a Show clearly on the diagram below the impact of a 15% increase in the price of tickets to a rock concert from an original price of $50. Label the change fully.

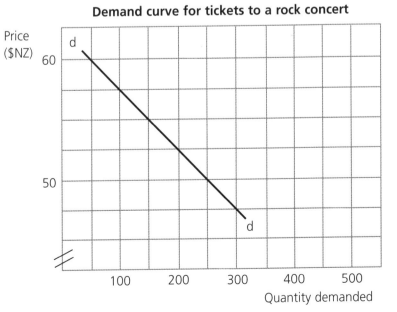

Demand curve for tickets to a rock concert

b Give two causes of a shift of the demand curve to the right apart from a decrease in income tax.

(i) _____

_____

_____

_____

(ii) _____

_____

_____

c Show an increase in demand by 50%. Label the change fully.

10 Zoe is a consumer of goat's milk. She is willing to buy 12 litres of goat's milk at $1.00 per litre. If the price rose to $1.50 per litre, Zoe would buy 8 litres. Zoe would purchase 2 litres if the price was $3 per litre, but would only buy 6 litres if the price fell to $2 per litre. At $0.50 per litre Zoe would buy 16 litres each month.

a Use the information to construct Zoe's demand schedule for goat's milk each month in the space below.

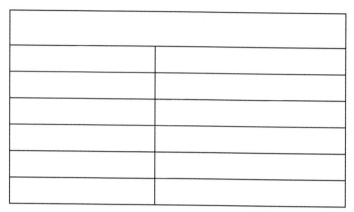

b Use the information above to draw Zoe's demand curve for goat's milk each month.

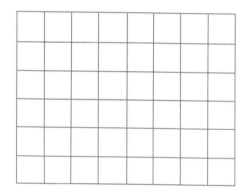

c Show on the graph how Zoe would react to a decrease in the price of goat's milk from $2.00 per litre to $1.00 per litre.

d Describe the effect of a change in the price of goat's milk from $2.00 per litre to $1.00 per litre.

_____

_____

_____

e If the price decreases from $2.00 per litre to $1.00 per litre, explain the effect on consumer spending.

_____

_____

_____

_____

f Zoe's demand for goat's milk each month falls by 50%. Show this decrease in demand on the graph you have drawn.

 ISBN: 9780170415972

11 When customers buy a motorbike, they usually buy protective clothing as well.

a What is the economic term used for items normally purchased together? _____

b What is the economic term used for items that might be bought in place of each other?

_____

c Charlotte-Rose works at the local supermarket. She is saving up to buy a new motorbike, but she is having trouble deciding which motorbike she wants to buy. Identify two factors that may affect Charlotte-Rose's demand for motorbikes.

(i) _____

(ii) _____

d Why might price not be the most important factor in Charlotte-Rose's decision?

_____

_____

_____

_____

_____

_____

e One brand of motorbike has a reputation for poor quality. Explain how that might affect consumer demand.

_____

_____

_____

_____

f Explain how a decrease in the price of a motorbike would affect the demand for motorbike helmets. Show the changes in the sketch diagrams below.

_____

_____

_____

_____

_____

_____

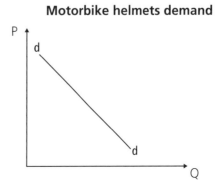

Motorbike demand

Motorbike helmets demand

12 a Complete Diagrams two and three given the change indicated in Diagram one.

(i) New cars   **Petrol**   **Secondhand cars**

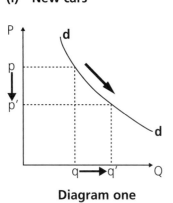

Diagram one

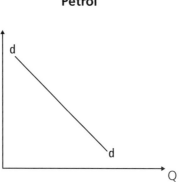

Diagram two

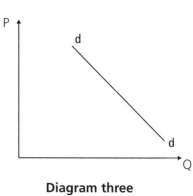

Diagram three

b Explain the difference between a **substitute** and a **complement**. Use examples related to cars.

_____

_____

_____

_____

c Explain the effect of a decrease in price for new cars on the demand for secondhand cars.

_____

_____

_____

_____

d Explain several flow-on effects a decrease in the price of a new car may have on a consumer.

_____

_____

_____

_____

_____

_____

_____

_____

_____

_____

_____

_____

13 Carefully label each diagram to show the changes indicated.

a A price increase of 20% from an original price of $25.

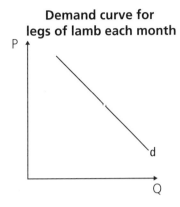

Demand curve for legs of lamb each month

b A price decrease of 25% from an original price of $120.

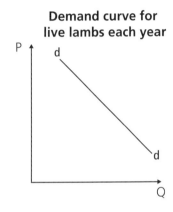

Demand curve for live lambs each year

c A 50% decrease in the demand for lambs due to a price decrease for beef.

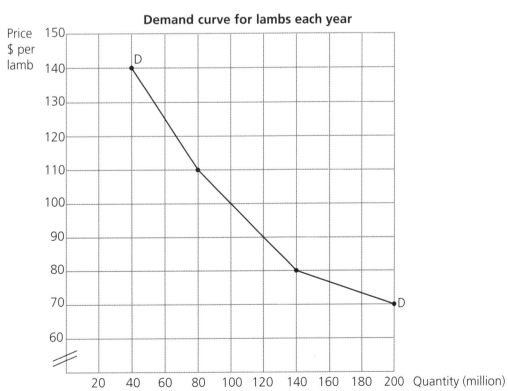

Demand curve for lambs each year

14 **a** A decrease in demand for pizza is not the same as a decrease in quantity demanded of pizza. Fully explain the statement. In your answer:

- Complete the sketch graph indicated by the title on each graph.
- Explain the reasons for a decrease in demand for pizza.
- Explain the reasons for a decrease in quantity demanded of pizza.

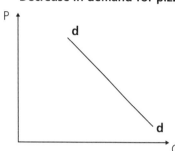

Decrease in demand for pizza

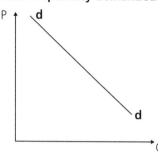

Decrease in quantity demanded for pizza

----

b Rose buys pizza or sushi. Discuss how an increase in the price of pizza might affect Rose's demand for sushi.

- Explain the relationship between pizza and sushi.
- Explain the effect on sushi when the price of pizza increases.
- Explain several flow-on effects this change may have for Rose.

   ISBN: 9780170415972

15 a Hal sometimes picks up a pizza when he hires a DVD rental movie each week.
Fully explain Hal's economic decisions based on the information. In your answer:
- Complete the sketch graph for pizza below to help clarify your explanation.
- Explain the relationship between a fall in the price of a DVD rental movie and pizza.
- Explain the effect of the decrease in price of DVD rentals on Hal's demand for pizza.

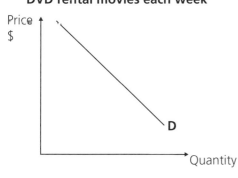

Hal's demand curve for DVD rental movies each week

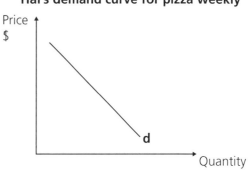

Hal's demand curve for pizza weekly

b Explain the effect a rise in income would have on Hal's demand for rental movies and pizza.

Review (exam) questions

With increased competition, the price of airline flights to various destinations around the country has fallen. This has had an impact on car rentals.

1 On the graphs below, discuss the extract above. In your answer you should:
- explain the relationship between domestic airline flights and car rentals
- show the changes in the sketch diagrams below
- explain several flow-on effects the change in demand for flights and car rentals will have for a consumer.

Demand for airline flights

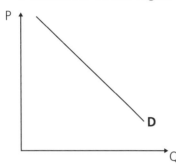

Demand for car rentals

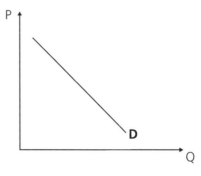

       ISBN: 9780170415972

The DVD rental industry is putting pressure on movies because they are lowering the price of DVDs.

2 Fully explain the effect of falling prices for DVD rental movies on Eleanor's demand for tickets to the movies. In your answer you should:
- explain the term that describes the relationship between movie tickets and DVD rentals
- fully label the graphs provided to show the changes and refer to them in your explanation
- explain several flow-on effects this change in demand may have for Eleanor.

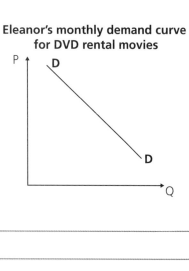

Eleanor's monthly demand curve for DVD rental movies

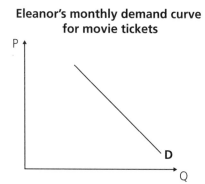

Eleanor's monthly demand curve for movie tickets

_____

_____

_____

_____

_____

_____

_____

_____

_____

_____

_____

_____

_____

_____

_____

_____

_____

_____

_____

_____

_____

_____

_____

_____

Adrian enjoys skateboarding or fishing when he is not working.

3 Discuss how a decrease in the price of fishing rods will affect Adrian's demand for skateboarding accessories. In your answer you should:
- show changes in the sketch graphs below and refer to them in your explanation
- explain the relationship between skateboarding accessories and fishing rods for Adrian
- explain several flow-on effects this change in demand could have for Adrian.

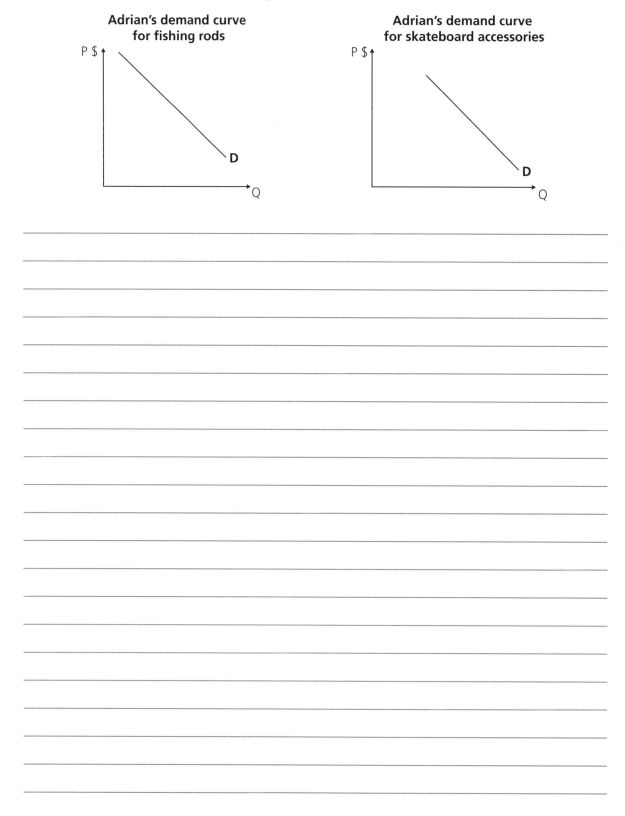

Adrian's demand curve for fishing rods

Adrian's demand curve for skateboard accessories

The local golf club has recently raised its membership fees.

4 Fully explain the effect of an increase in the price of golf club membership on the demand for golf coaching. In your answer you should:

- show the effects of an increase in the price of golf club membership on the demand for golf coaching
- explain the relationship between golf club membership and golf coaching
- explain the effect of an increase in the price of golf club membership on golf coaching. Refer to your graphs
- explain several flow-on effects for consumers.

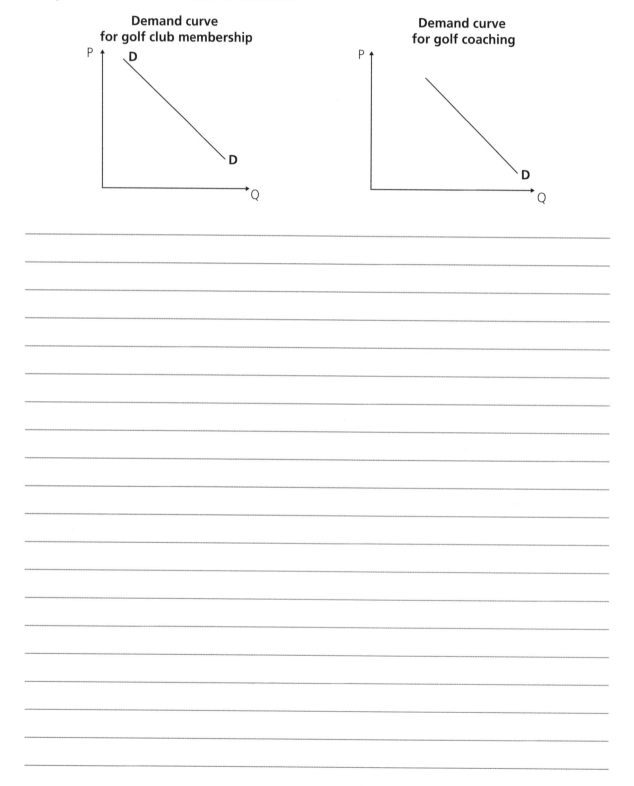

5 DEMAND
Types of goods and services

Household income (Y)

A **household** is either a person or a group of people living under one roof. A household's income (Y) comes from supplying labour (human) resources to firms in return for wages. **Disposable income** is income after direct (income) taxes are paid and any transfers received. When direct (income) tax rates are cut or transfers increase then disposable incomes rise.

A household can either spend or save the income they receive. **Consumption spending (C)** is household spending on goods and services and is likely to increase when incomes rise. **Savings (S)** represents **income not spent** (it involves **abstaining from consumption**). The level of savings a household has will depend on several factors including interest rates, expectations about the future and attitudes towards thrift. Individuals may save more if they are concerned about the future and desire to have funds for an emergency, such as an unexpected bill for repairs to a house or car. As interest rates increase individuals are likely to save more because they are receiving a higher return on funds put aside to use later.

A household's **discretionary income** is a household's disposable income minus all essential payments required. Essential payments would include items such as mortgage repayments, insurance, rates, groceries. utilities such as power and water, and other necessities. What is left over from a household's disposable income after other commitments are accounted for is a household's discretionary income. The remaining income can either be used for additional spending or can be saved. When interest rates paid on a variable mortgage fall then a household will pay less for its mortgage, this will result in an increase in discretionary income rather than disposable income.

Household consumption patterns

A person's level of **consumption** is lower than their level of **income** because income tax (Pay As You Earn) is deducted from income and some income is saved (not spent). The graph shows that as income rises, so will consumption, and as income falls, so will consumption, that is, changes in consumption follow changes in income.

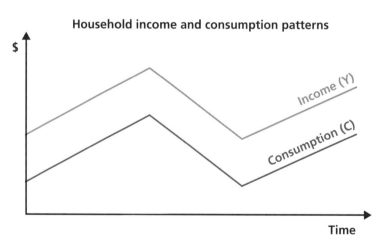

Household income and consumption patterns

Income (Y)

Consumption (C)

Time

As people's income changes the types of goods and services they purchase will also change. At lower levels of income a higher proportion of a consumer's income is spent on necessities, cheaper alternatives or inferior goods. As income rises consumption of necessities like food, clothing and shelter will increase and eventually level off. Also as income rises consumers will probably buy fewer inferior goods such as cheap cuts of meat or second-hand clothing. At higher levels of income a higher proportion of income is spent on luxuries such as overseas travel or fashionable clothes.

Saving is a consumer's income that is not spent and as a household's income rises the percentage of household income saved is likely to increase because more income means more saving is possible. The percentage of income consumed is therefore likely to decrease.

      ISBN: 9780170415972

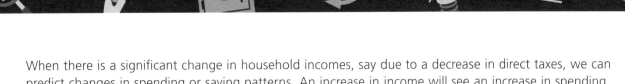

When there is a significant change in household incomes, say due to a decrease in direct taxes, we can predict changes in spending or saving patterns. An increase in income will see an increase in spending on luxuries and greater savings. An economic downturn (or recession), where household incomes fall, is likely to see a fall in spending on luxuries and reduced savings.

Inferior goods

Inferior goods are **low quality** goods and services that individuals buy (demand) less of as their income increases, e.g., opportunity shop clothes, cheap cuts of meat, cheap cars, budget brand food items at a supermarket and cask wine.

The graph shows the relationship between the quantity demanded of an inferior good and income. As the level of household income increases the total dollars spent on inferior goods will decrease because households are able to afford better quality or normal

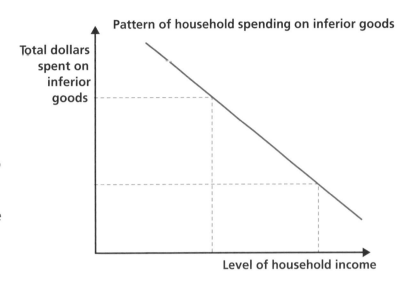

goods. Households change from buying budget brands to better quality goods and services.

Normal goods

Normal goods are goods and services that individuals will buy (demand) more of as their income increases or demand less of as their income decreases. Normal goods may be necessities or luxuries.

Necessities

Necessities are goods and services individuals must have in order to **sustain life**, such as food, clothes or shelter and water.

The graph shows the relationship between the quantity demanded of necessities and income. As the level of household income increases the total dollars spent on necessities increases a small amount. The amount spent on necessities does not increase that much since households will

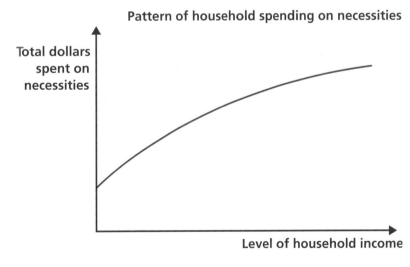

spend their income on other goods and services.

Household spending on necessities reaches a saturation point since there is only so much that needs to be spent on food, clothing and housing. Household spending will increase slightly because households buy better-quality clothing, food and housing.

Luxuries

Luxuries are goods and services that **make life more comfortable and enjoyable**, e.g., new cars, first class airline tickets, a Rolex watch, Wagyu beef, overseas travel and entertainment. Luxuries are often considered to be an indulgence rather than a necessity. The proportion of household income spent on necessities tends to level off at higher levels of income, an increasing proportion of income will be spent on luxury goods and services.

The graph shows that at low levels of income, there is no spending on luxuries because households are unable to afford it, all household income is spent on necessities or inferior goods. As income rises, so does spending on luxuries because households can now afford to buy more than just their necessities. At high levels of income, spending on luxuries can level off because individuals' desires are not so great. In this scenario they start to save more.

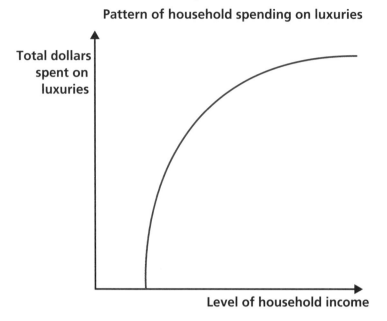

Pattern of household spending on luxuries

Spending on luxury goods and services is often associated with affluence.

Luxury goods and services are more expensive and are expected to last longer than other similar goods because they are high quality items made from better material or components.

Changes in consumption spending

A change in **households' attitudes** can influence consumption spending, for example, households may decide to reduce levels of debt. An increase in income that arises from direct tax cuts may see little change in consumption spending because the additional disposable income households receive is used to pay back loans.

Consumer confidence can influence the level of consumption spending. If households are more concerned about the future they may decide to save more and reduce consumption spending. As more households participate in (or join) savings schemes and/or increase their contributions then consumption spending will decrease.

Consumption spending is likely to increase if **household disposable incomes** (HDI) increase. When household disposable incomes increase they can afford more. Household disposable incomes will increase if direct (income) taxes are cut and/or transfer payments are increased.

If **interest rates** fall there is less incentive for households to save, because they get a lower return and this will discourage savings therefore consumption spending will increase. If interest rates fall then it is possible that households will get a loan to buy items they desire (whiteware, cars, furniture) or to do renovations to homes or buy a property (home), this will increase consumption spending.

If property and house prices increase then households may be encouraged to borrow more from banks and financial instutions by asking for a loan based on the increased equity they have in their home or property, this is known as the **wealth effect**. As borrowed funds are spent on goods and services consumption spending will increase.

Key terms and ideas

Household	A person or group of individuals (family, flatting situation, couple) who are living under one roof.
The relationship between income and types of goods and services purchased	• At lower levels of income a high proportion of income is spent on necessities/inferior goods. • At higher levels of income a higher proportion of income is spent on luxuries
Total dollars spent on inferior goods 0 Level of household income	• Inferior goods are low quality goods and services that households demand less of when income rises. • Trend: As income increases the total dollars spent on inferior goods will decrease. • Reasons: Households are able to afford better quality or normal goods. Households change from buying budget brands to better quality goods and services.
Total dollars spent on necessities 0 Level of household income	• Necessities are goods and services households must have in order to sustain life, such as food, clothes or shelter and water. • Trend: As income increases the total dollars spent on necessities increases a small amount. • Reasons: The amount spent on necessities does not increase that much since households will spend their income on other goods. There is only so much you need to spend on food/clothing/housing. Household spending on necessities will increase slightly as households buy better quality clothes/food/housing.
Total dollars spent on luxuries 0 Level of household income	• Luxuries are goods and services that make life more comfortable and enjoyable but households could manage without them. • Trend: At low levels of income there is no income spent on luxuries. As household income increases so does spending on luxuries. • Reasons: At low levels of income, there is no household spending on luxuries because households are unable to afford it. As income increases, so does spending on luxuries because households can now afford to buy more than just necessities.
Savings	That part of income that is not spent, e.g., buying shares or putting funds in to a term deposit.
Disposable income	Household income after government taxes and transfers are taken into account.

Student notes: Demand – Types of goods and services

 ISBN: 9780170415972

QUESTIONS & TASKS

1 **a** Define the term "luxuries".

_____

_____

_____

_____

_____

_____

_____

_____

_____

_____

b Explain why as income increases consumption of necessities will increase slightly and tend to level off, while consumption of inferior goods will decline.

_____

_____

_____

_____

_____

_____

_____

_____

_____

_____

c What is the likely impact on the respective percentages of household income saved and consumed when income falls? Explain why this occurs.

_____

_____

_____

_____

_____

_____

Ashley will often grab a pizza with friends, while at other times they will go out to an upmarket restaurant.

2 a Complete the sketch graphs below to show the effect a fall in direct tax rates would have on Ashley's demand for meals out.

Ashley's demand for pizza

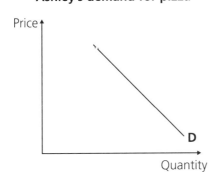

Ashley's demand for restaurant meals

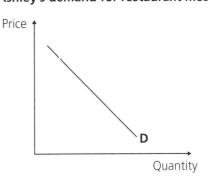

b (i) Explain the link between a decrease in direct tax rates and disposable income.

(ii) Explain luxury goods and inferior goods in Ashley's context. Refer to your graphs.

(iii) Explain a possible flow-on effect this change may have for Ashley.

_____
_____
_____
_____
_____
_____
_____
_____
_____
_____
_____
_____
_____
_____
_____
_____
_____
_____
_____
_____
_____
_____
_____

3 For many households most of their disposable income is spent on necessities like food, electricity and health services. Little is left over for luxuries like new cars, overseas holidays or going out.

a Define the term household.

_____

_____

b Define the term necessities and explain why a cellphone might be considered a necessity.

_____

_____

_____

_____

c Explain why the disposable household income is less than the total amount the family earns.

_____

_____

d The household's main caregiver returns to full-time work now that all their children are attending school. This will lift the income of the household. Explain how this will affect the household consumption patterns, with specific reference to necessities and luxuries.

_____

_____

_____

_____

_____

_____

_____

_____

_____

_____

_____

_____

_____

e (i) What is meant by the term 'savings'?

_____

(ii) As household income increases explain why they can now save.

_____

_____

_____

_____

_____

4   Study the table below and answer the questions that follow.

Household and income	Food	Housing	Transport	Apparel	Other goods & services	Household operation	Savings
Percentage of monthly expenditure							
A $5 000	14	18	17	3	25	12	11
B $2 000	18	13	18	2	26	16	7

a   Which items does Household B spend more on each month than Household A?   _____

b   Use the data above to analyse how each of the factors below will change **as income decreases**.
    Give a reason for each change.

   (i)   The percentage of income saved: _____

   _____

   _____

   (ii) The percentage of income spent:_____

   _____

c   Why does the percentage of income spent on food **rise** as income decreases?

   _____

   _____

   _____

d   Define the term luxuries.

   _____

   _____

e   Define disposable income.

   _____

   _____

   _____

   _____

f   Explain the effect of a decrease in interest rates on a household's disposable income and/or
    discretionary income.

   _____

   _____

   _____

   _____

   _____

   _____

   _____

   _____

5 The table reflects a typical household's level of spending for each item as their income increases over time.

A typical family's spending as income increases			
Item	Before	Now	Future
Food	24%	16%	15%
Housing	39%	29%	25%
Clothing	17%	18%	20%
Savings	0%	10%	20%

a Which item does the family spend the most on **now**? _____

b Why does the total for **now** not equal 100%?

_____

c Explain the changes expected for each item as their household income increases.

(i) Food: _____

_____

(ii) Housing: _____

_____

_____

(iii) Clothing: _____

_____

(iv) Savings: _____

d On the axes provided below, carefully sketch the pattern of spending on necessities as household income increases.

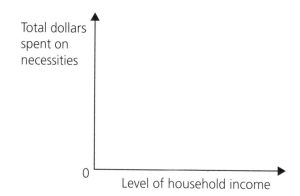

6 Study the table below and answer the questions that follow.

Spending patterns for household X			
Stage of life	Income ($)	Consumption ($)	Savings ($)
A	0	8 000	–
B	10 000	9 900	100
C	100 000	90 000	10 000

a Even when household X earns no income, they still spend money on goods and services. How can they do this?

_____

_____

b Use the data above to analyse how each of the factors below will change as income increases. Give a reason for each change.

(i) The percentage of income spent: _____

_____

(ii) The percentage of income saved: _____

_____

c Why does the percentage of income spent on food fall as income increases?

_____

_____

_____

d (i) On the axes provided, carefully sketch the pattern of spending on inferior goods as household income increases.

(ii) Provide a reason for the change in spending on inferior goods as household income increases.

_____

_____

_____

_____

_____

_____

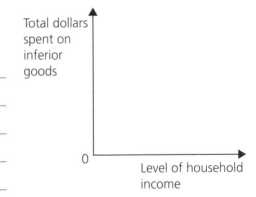

e The government has recently announced a cut in direct (income) tax rates. Identify and explain what effect the cut in direct (income) tax rates will have on each of the following.

(i) Proportion of income saved by households.

Effect: _____ Explanation: _____

_____

(ii) Proportion of luxury goods sold in retail shops.

Effect: _____ Explanation: _____

_____

Review (exam) questions

As part of his job, Tau has to travel to various locations around the city. When he was a junior in the office he caught a bus. Now that he has earned a promotion he catches a taxi. He is planning to use a limousine when he becomes a partner in the business next month.

1 Discuss the effect that an increase in Tau's income and a change in his circumstances in the business would have on his demand for various modes of transport. In your answer you should:
   • use economic terms to describe different modes of transport available to Tau
   • explain how and why his mode of transport could change
   • explain several flow-on effects this change in demand may have on Tau.

_____

_____

_____

_____

_____

_____

_____

_____

_____

_____

_____

_____

_____

_____

_____

_____

_____

_____

_____

_____

_____

_____

_____

_____

_____

_____

Ryan has just been made redundant from his workplace.

2 Discuss the effect a fall in Ryan's income has on his demand for branded beachwear and non-branded beachwear. In your answer you should:
- show the changes in the sketch diagrams below
- use appropriate economic terms to describe branded beachwear and non-branded beachwear for Ryan
- refer to the graphs in your explanation
- explain flow-on effects these changes in demand may have for Ryan.

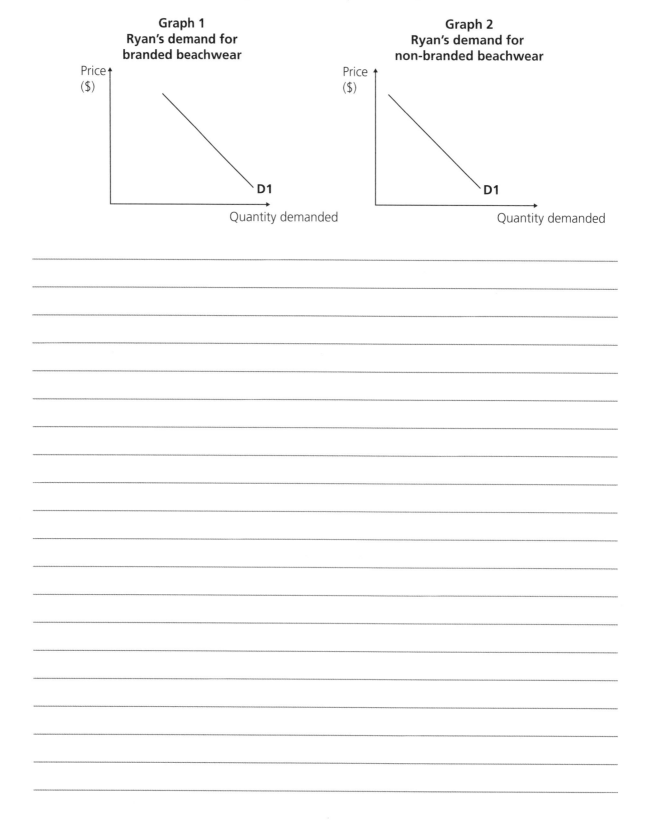

_____
_____
_____
_____
_____
_____
_____
_____
_____
_____
_____
_____
_____
_____
_____
_____
_____
_____
_____
_____

     ISBN: 9780170415972

6 SUPPLY
Basic concepts

Supply, supply schedules and the law of supply

Supply is the quantity of a good or service a supplier will willingly bring to the market at a range of prices.

A **supply schedule** is a table of figures that relates the price to the quantity a supplier will bring to the market. The information in a supply schedule assumes that all other factors that may influence supply are held constant. The Latin term **ceteris paribus** describes this assumption of holding all other factors unchanged. This allows us to clearly see the relationship between price and quantity supplied.

Nature's Product supply schedule for organic chicken each month	
Price $ per kg	Quantity supplied (000 kgs)
5	5
10	10
20	20

To construct or draw up a supply schedule, certain conventions (or rules) are followed. These are a title that includes the name of the supplier, what is supplied and in what time period. A heading of price in the left hand column with units. A heading of Quantity Supplied in the right hand column with units. Figures in either ascending or descending order accurately reflecting the information from a graph or resource material.

The **law of supply** states that as the price of a good or service increases, the quantity supplied increases, ceteris paribus. Or, as the price of a good or service decreases, the quantity supplied decreases, ceteris paribus. As the **price** of a good or service **increases quantity supplied increases** because selling the good or providing that service becomes relatively more profitable for a firm because the revenue (income) it earns is higher and it will be more able to cover costs. A firm will increase quantity supplied to maximise profits.

As the **price** of a good or service **decreases the quantity supplied decreases** because selling the good or providing that service becomes relatively less profitable for a firm because the revenue (income) it earns is lower and it will be less able to cover costs. As price falls a firm might increase the production of a related good, close down if the revenue it earns is insufficient to cover costs or decide to use its resources in another way.

Related goods and services are the different types of output that producers can make using the inputs (resources) used in the production process. Producers will tend to switch resources into the production of the good or service with the higher price, and decrease output of the other good or service. For example, bread rolls and a bread loaf require similar ingredients (flour, water and salt) and resources to make, such as the ovens, power and workers. As the price of bread rolls increases then quantity supplied of bread rolls increases, ceteris paribus. As the price of bread rolls increases a firm will switch resources into producing bread rolls because it is relatively more profitable because the firm is earning higher revenue and is more able to cover costs. The supply of loaves of bread (the related product) decreases because the firm has fewer resources available to make bread loaves because it is relatively less profitable to do so.

Price and cost

Price is determined by the market forces of demand and supply and is how much a customer will pay in order to have the good or service. Price is what a firm receives from the sale of a good or the provision of a service to its clients (customers). **Cost** is how much it takes for a firm to either get a good produced or service ready to sell in the market. Costs include all the inputs used in the production process such as raw materials, power, office expenses and wages.

    ISBN: 9780170415972

Drawing a supply curve

A supply curve shows the information from a supply schedule or resource material graphically.

When drawing a supply curve certain conventions or rules that should be followed are listed beside the supply curve for Nature's organic chicken. Note that the price is on the Y (vertical) axis and the quantity supplied is on the X (horizontal) axis.

The **supply curve slopes up to the right** because as the price of a good

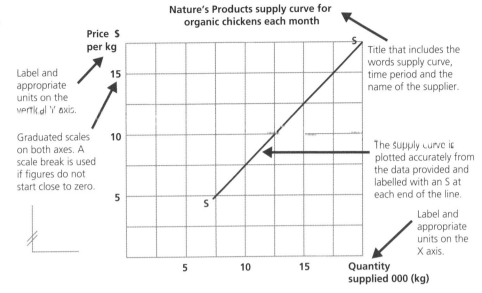

Nature's Products supply curve for organic chickens each month

Title that includes the words supply curve, time period and the name of the supplier.

Label and appropriate units on the vertical Y axis.

Graduated scales on both axes. A scale break is used if figures do not start close to zero.

The supply curve is plotted accurately from the data provided and labelled with an S at each end of the line.

Label and appropriate units on the X axis.

or service increases the quantity supplied will increase because this enables a firm to increase their revenue (returns) and/or profit.

A supply curve shows that price and quantity have a direct relationship, i.e. that price and quantity supplied are positively related.

A movement along a supply curve

If there is a change 'only' in the **price** of a good itself, there is a **movement along** a supply curve and a **change in quantity supplied**.

To show a price change (movement along) a supply curve, label the original price P or P1 and the original quantity supplied Q or Q1. The new price is labelled P' or P2 and the new quantity supplied is labelled Q' or Q2. Direction arrows are used to show the direction of the change in price and quantity supplied, from the original position to the new position. Dotted lines are used to show the appropriate points on the supply curve to the price and quantity axes.

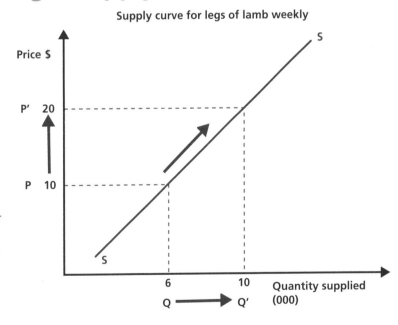

Supply curve for legs of lamb weekly

The supply curve shows an increase in price from $10 (P) to $20 (P') which results in an increase in quantity supplied from 6 000 (Q) to 10 000 (Q').

An increase in price causes an increase in quantity supplied, illustrated by a movement up the existing supply curve to the right. A decrease in price causes a decrease in quantity supplied, illustrated by a movement down the supply curve to the left.

A **firm's revenue** is the value of total sales which equals the price of each item multiplied by the quantity of each item sold. In the diagram the revenue increases from $60 000 ($10 multiplied by 6 000) to $200 000 ($20 multiplied by 10 000).

Key terms and ideas

Ceteris paribus	All other factors (not price) being equal/held constant.
Law of supply	An increase in the price of a good or service will lead to an increase in the quantity supplied, ceteris paribus (or vice versa).
Supply (individual)	Amount of a good or service *one* firm is willing and able to supply at various prices.
Show a price change on a supply curve	Your graph MUST have arrows, be fully labelled and be accurate.
The cause of a movement along a supply curve	A change in the price of the product only (will cause a change in quantity supplied).
Reasons why firms supply less at lower prices	• Insufficient profit means the firm couldn't cover costs of production. • Reduced profits mean the firm decides to use resources in another way.
Reasons why firms supply more as price increases	• Costs increase so a higher price needed. • To make higher profits or revenue. • Increased scarcity of resources so a higher price needed.
A firm's revenue is ...	Value of total sales which equals the price of each item multiplied by the quantity of each item sold.
Related good and service	Different types of output that producers can make using the inputs (resources) used in the production process.

Student notes: Supply – Basic concepts

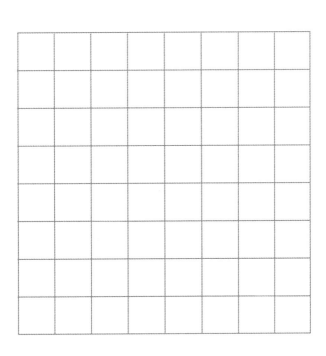

ISBN: 9780170415972

QUESTIONS & TASKS

1 **a** Draw the supply curve for paperback books given the schedule below.

Supply schedule for paperback books each month	
Price $ per book	Quantity supplied
4	1 000
12	5 000
24	7 000

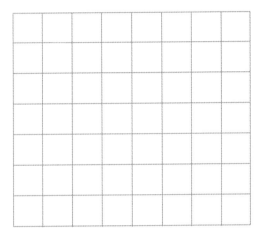

b How many books (according to your graph) are supplied at $8? _____

c Explain how the supply curve illustrates the law of supply.

_____

_____

d Define individual supply.

_____

_____

_____

e Describe the effects of a change in price of paperback books each month from $4 per book to $10 per book.

_____

_____

f Explain the flow-on effects on the firm of an increase in price from $4 per book to $10 per book.

_____

_____

_____

2 Steve's pizza firm sells pizza as well as garlic bread. The price of pizza has recently increased by 100%. Study the graph and answer the questions that follow.

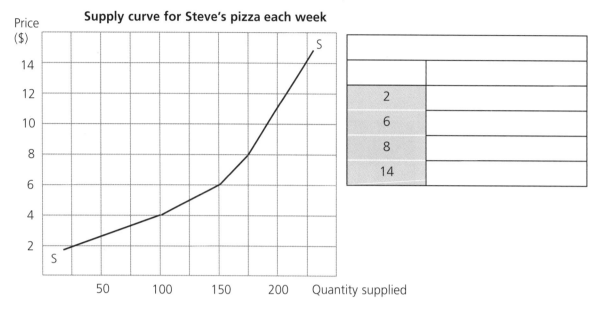

2	
6	
8	
14	

a Complete the empty boxes in the table above using your knowledge and the correct information from the graph.

b Show on the graph how Steve's decision-making as a producer may react to an increase in the price of pizza from $4 by 100%.

c (i) Describe the law of supply by referring to the relevant data above.

_____

_____

_____

_____

_____

(ii) Explain the law of supply

_____

_____

_____

_____

(iii) Explain the effect the rising price of pizza has on Steve's supply of garlic bread.

_____

_____

_____

_____

_____

 ISBN: 9780170415972

3 Sam sells apples at the local farmers' market. His supply schedule is shown below.

a Using the axes provided below, draw Sam's supply curve for organic apples. Fully label your graph.

Sam's supply schedule for organic apples each week	
Price ($) per apple	Quantity supplied
0.20	25
0.40	100
0.60	150
1.00	175
1.60	200

b What is supply?

c What does ceteris paribus mean?

d The price increases from $0.40 per apple to $0.60 per apple. Discuss the law of supply by referring to the data.

e Fully explain what Sam might do if the price per apple falls below $0.20 per apple.

4 a In Economics, what is the name given to the table below? _____

Morris Ltd supply of chicken per week		
Price ($ per kg)	Quantity supplied (kg)	Revenue $
0.70	2000	
0.90	2500	
1.10	3000	
1.30	3500	

b Draw the information from the table in the grid below.

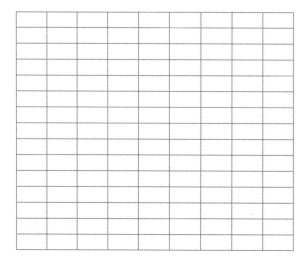

c (i) Show the effect of a price decrease from $1.30 per kg to $0.90 per kg.

(ii) Describe the effect of a change in the price of chicken from $1.30 per kg to $0.90 per kg.

_____

_____

d Explain what is meant by individual supply.

_____

_____

_____

_____

e (i) Use the column in the table above to calculate the firm's revenue at each price.

(ii) Explain why the supply curve slopes up to the right.

_____

_____

_____

5 **a** What is the name given to the table of figures below? _____

b Use the information from the table below to graph the supply curve for Taylor's Ice Cream each month on the grid provided. Label your diagram fully.

Supply of Taylor's Ice Cream each month		
Price ($ per litre)	Quantity (000 litres)	Revenue ($)
0.50	10	
1.00	17	
1.50	20	
2.00	23	
2.50	24	

c Show on the graph you have drawn above a price decrease from $2.00 per litre to $1.00 per litre.

d Use the column in the table above to calculate the firm's revenue at each price.

e Describe the law of supply.

_____

_____

f Explain why Taylor's Ice cream will not supply any ice cream when the price is $0.25 per litre.

_____

_____

_____

6 Billy is the owner of a goat herd. He is willing to supply 10 litres of goats' milk at $1.00 per litre. If the price rose to $1.50 per litre, Billy would supply 15 litres per day. Billy would supply 20 litres if the price was $3 per litre, but would only supply 17.5 litres if the price fell to $2 per litre. At $0.50 per litre Billy would supply 2.5 litres each day.

a Use the information to construct Billy's supply schedule for goats' milk for each day in the space below.

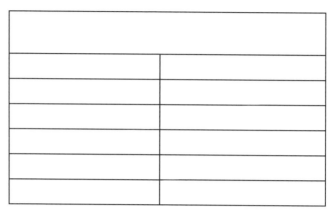

b Use the information above to draw Billy's supply curve for goats' milk per day.

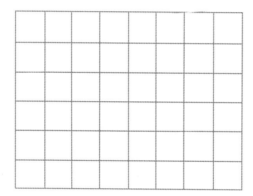

c Show on the graph how Billy would react to a decrease in the price of goats' milk from $2.00 per litre to $1.00 per litre.

d Describe the effect of a change in the price of goats' milk from $2.00 per litre to $1.00 per litre.

(i) _____

_____

(ii) Identify the change in revenue for Billy. The decrease in price has led to a _____ of _____ dollars.

e Explain why producers supply more goats' milk as the price increases.

_____

_____

_____

_____

7 **a** Draw a supply curve of the table in the grid below.

National Coal supply schedule for coal each year	
Price ($ per tonne)	Quantity supplied (000 tonnes)
300	5
500	20
700	30
800	35

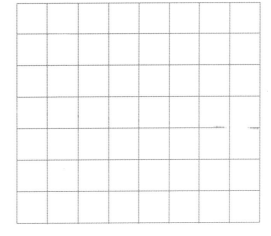

b **(i)** Show a price change from $500 per tonne to $600 per tonne.

(ii) Identify the change in quantity.
The increase in price has led to an

_____ of 5 000 _____

(ii) Identify the change in revenue for National Coal.
The increase in price has led to an _____

of _____ dollars.

(iii) Explain a flow-on effect of this change on National's business operation.

_____

_____

_____

_____

c Explain why the supply curve slopes up to the right.

_____

_____

_____

_____

_____

d What is supply?

_____

_____

e Fully explain why National Coal will not supply any coal when the price is $200 per tonne.

_____

_____

_____

_____

_____

Review (exam) questions

Price and quantity supplied have a positive relationship.

1 Explain the relationship between price and quantity supplied. In your answer you should:
- describe what is meant by 'supply'
- draw a supply curve using the schedule opposite and the grid provided
- show a price decrease from $2.00 per muffin of 25% and give reasons for the change in the quantity of muffins supplied
- explain several flow-on effects of the price change for Joe.

Joe's supply schedule for muffins each month	
Price ($)	Quantity supplied (000)
0.50	1
1.00	6
2.00	9
3.00	10

Steve's firm produces ice cream or yoghurt.

2 Fully explain the law of supply in the context of Steve's supply schedule for ice cream.
In your answer you should:
- draw a fully labelled supply curve using the information from the supply schedule. Show the effect of the price of ice cream increasing from $1.00 per litre by 100%
- discuss the changes in the supply of ice cream as the price rises from $1.00 by 100% by referring to the law of supply. Give reasons for the change in the quantity of ice cream Steve may supply
- explain flow-on effects this price change may have for Steve.

Steve's supply schedule for ice cream each week	
Price ($) per litre	Quantity supplied (litres)
0.50	0
1.00	80
1.50	140
3.00	260

PHOTOCOPYING OF THIS PAGE IS RESTRICTED UNDER LAW.   ISBN: 9780170415972

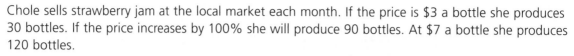

Chole sells strawberry jam at the local market each month. If the price is $3 a bottle she produces 30 bottles. If the price increases by 100% she will produce 90 bottles. At $7 a bottle she produces 120 bottles.

3 Use the information above to draw a supply curve in the grid below. Show the effect of a price decrease of 33.3% from $6.00 per bottle for Chole's strawberry jam. Fully label the changes. Discuss the law of supply as it relates to a decrease in price. In your answer you should:
- describe the law of supply by referring to relevant data from your graph
- fully explain the effect of a price decrease
- fully explain what Chole might do if the price for her strawberry jam falls below $3 a bottle.

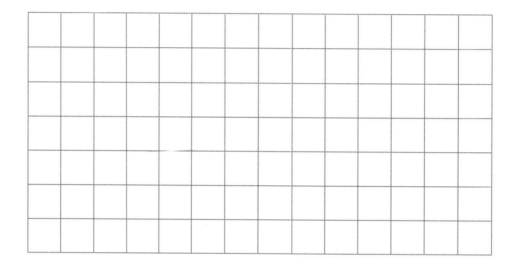

_____
_____
_____
_____
_____
_____
_____
_____
_____
_____
_____
_____
_____
_____
_____
_____

ISBN: 9780170415972

4 Price and quantity supplied have a direct relationship.

Explain the relationship between price and quantity supplied. In your answer you should:

- draw a supply curve using the schedule opposite and the grid provided
- show a price increase from $500 per house to $1 000 per house
- describe the law of supply by referring to the graph provided
- explain the concept of ceteris paribus in the context of the law of supply
- explain a reason for the law of supply
- explain a flow-on effect this change in supply may have on Ernie's resource use.

Ernie's supply schedule for house washes each week	
Price ($) per house	Quantity supplied (houses)
250	2
500	5
1 000	7
1 500	10

7 SUPPLY
Conditions/shifts

Price and cost

It is important to distinguish between the terms "price" and "costs" for a firm. **Price** is determined by the market forces of demand and supply and is how much a customer will pay in order to have the good or service. Price is what a firm receives from the sale of a good or the provision of a service to its clients (customers). **Cost** is how much it takes for a firm to either get a good produced or service ready to sell in the market. Costs include all the inputs used in the production process such as raw materials, power, office expenses and wages. Therefore, cost and price are not the same thing.

Conditions of supply

A change in the price of a good or service causes a **movement along** an existing supply curve and a **change in quantity supplied**. A change in **conditions or determinants of supply** cause a supply curve to **shift** to an entirely new position, either inward (to the left) or outward (to the right) and a **change in supply**. Conditions or determinants of supply include costs of production, productivity, indirect tax, subsidies, the price of a related good, a tariff and if there is a good or bad growing season.

Shifts of the supply curve

When we relax the assumption ceteris paribus the supply curve will shift to an entirely new position or a new supply schedule will be drawn up. At each and every price there is a new quantity supplied.

A shift of the supply curve **outward (to the right)** is termed an **increase in supply**, this means that at each and every price there is an increase in quantity supplied. A shift of the supply curve **inward (to the left)** is termed a **decrease in supply**, this means that at each and every price there is a decrease in quantity supplied.

The new supply curve is drawn parallel to the original supply curve and labelled S´or S2. Arrows are used to show the direction of the shift of the curve. The increase in supply can be illustrated in a supply schedule or supply curve as shown.

The factors **(conditions or determinants of supply)** that will cause the supply curve to shift include the costs of production, workers productivity, indirect taxes, subsidies, the price of a related good, tariffs and if there is a good or bad growing season.

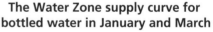

The Water Zone supply schedule for bottled water in January and March

Price $ per bottle	Quantity supplied January (bottles)	Quantity supplied March (bottles)
1.00	2000	3000
2.00	4000	5000
3.00	6000	7000

Note at each and every price there is an increase in quantity supplied which we term an increase in supply.

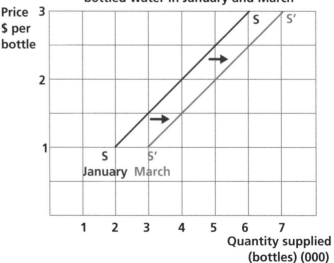

The Water Zone supply curve for bottled water in January and March

PHOTOCOPYING OF THIS PAGE IS RESTRICTED UNDER LAW.   ISBN: 9780170415972

Reasons for shifts

A change in a **cost of production** is the factor that will have the greatest bearing on supply for firms. Costs of production can include items like workers' wages, raw materials, power and transport costs. As costs of production fall, a firm is likely to put a larger quantity of the good or service on the market at any given price because it will become relatively more profitable for a supplier to produce that good or provide that service. This results in an outward (to the right) shift of the supply curve, indicating that there is an increase in the quantity supplied at each and every price.

Changes made by the government regarding either **indirect taxes** (GST, VAT) or giving a producer a **subsidy** will affect supply. An **indirect tax** is a tax that is collected by a third party and passed on to the government. If the rate of an indirect tax is raised, it will cause a firm's costs to increase and profits to decrease. Therefore, supply will decrease which indicates that at each and every price there is a decrease in quantity supplied. A **subsidy** is a payment by government to firms to keep costs down. Firms will switch resources into the good or service that has received the subsidy because as the costs of production fall it is more profitable to make the good or provide the service.

Related goods and services are the different types of output that producers can make using the inputs (resources) used in the production process. Producers will tend to switch resources into the production of the good or service with the higher price, and decrease output of the other good or service. For example, bread rolls and a bread loaf require similar ingredients (flour, water and salt) and resources to make, such as the ovens, power and workers. As the price of bread rolls increases then quantity supplied of bread rolls increases, ceteris paribus. As the price of bread rolls increases a firm will switch resources into producing bread rolls because it is relatively more profitable because the firm is earning higher revenue and is more able to cover costs. The supply of loaves of bread (the related product) decreases because the firm has fewer resources available to make bread loaves because it is relatively less profitable to do so.

Productivity is a measure of the output per worker or the output per machine. Changes in technology that impact on productivity change the quantity supplied by a firm at each and every price. An increase in productivity in the factory that uses new robot technology will mean that the production process is more efficient. Because the production process is more efficient a firm's costs of production fall. As costs of production decrease it will become more profitable for a supplier to produce a product. This will result in an increase in supply (at each and every price there will be an increase in quantity supplied and the supply curve will shift outward to the right).

A **tariff** is a tax placed (or levied) on imports, a tariff will increase costs of production because firms have to pay a higher price. As costs of production increase a firm is likely to put a smaller quantity of the good or service on the market at any given price, because it will become relatively less profitable for a supplier to produce that good or provide that service. Import licences or quotas restrict the quantity of imports in a given time period, therefore supply will decrease. If restrictions are lifted, an importer is more able to bring the product into the country which will increase supply.

The **number of firms** that exist in a market has a bearing on supply. If more firms enter a market to produce a good or provide a service this will add to the total capacity that is able to be produced and be made available causing supply to increase.

Implications of a shift of the supply curve

When the supply curve shifts to the right or the left it will have an impact on the firm in other ways. An increase in supply (a shift to the right) may mean the firm will need to hire and train new staff, require existing staff to work overtime, buy and install new machinery or look at shifting to larger premises.

A decrease in supply (a shift to the left) may mean the firm will have to lay off staff, reduce output of one product while increasing output of another product, or look at ways of reducing costs or possibly closing down.

External influences on supply

Environmental, trade, legal and political factors will influence the output decisions of firms.

Environmental factors – the extent to which a firm is concerned about environmental issues will influence the output decisions they make. A firm whose goal is to be environmentally friendly may take the time and expense to ensure the packaging of its products allows for recycling and reducing waste in its production process. For them the costs of production will increase and supply is decreased. Another firm in the same industry may not care and because using other methods of production is cheaper and less time consuming, the costs of production decrease and supply will increase.

Legal factors – firms have to operate within the legal framework of the country by following the laws (rules and regulations) determined by government. Anti-pollution laws, safety and health standards, labelling and packaging requirements are all legal factors that influence the output decisions of firms. Compliance with these rules and regulations, set by government or local councils, will in most instances increase the costs of production and supply will decrease.

Political factors – the government may attempt to discourage the use of certain products, such as cigarettes and alcohol, by placing a sales tax on them. This increases the costs of production and decreases the supply. By subsidising firms with a payment to help reduce the costs of production and increase supply the government can encourage output of certain goods and services. The government can promote and free up trade between nations by negotiating trade agreements with other nations. This decision by government will influence a firms' supply decisions.

Trade factors – firms as exporters and/or importers are influenced by trade factors. An importer of foreign-made goods may have a tariff (a tax on imports) placed on the product. This increases the costs to the firm and supply will decrease. The prevailing price for a good or service on the world market (world price) will affect a firm's output decisions. A rise in the world price may encourage local firms to increase the quantity supplied and export overseas.

Cultural factors – an awareness of being culturally sensitive and cultural issues will influence a firm's output decisions. For example, the need to seek local councils permission to carry out a planned development may increase costs and supply will decrease.

Key terms and ideas

What will cause the supply curve to shift?	Change in conditions (determinants) of supply.
Reasons for increase in supply (shift right) of supply curve Kids' clothes *[graph: Price vs Quantity supplied showing supply curve shifting right from S to S']*	• Costs of production decrease, e.g. lower wages for workers. • New technology. • Workers' productivity increases. • Indirect tax decreases, e.g. GST, sales tax. • Subsidy given by government. • Tax on imports (tariffs) lifted by government. • Price of related good decreases – e.g. if the price received for adult clothes falls, the firm will make more kids' clothes.
Reason for decrease in supply (shift left) of supply curve Kids' clothes *[graph: Price vs Quantity supplied showing supply curve shifting left from S to S']*	• Costs of production increase, e.g. higher wages for workers. • Workers' productivity decreases. • Indirect tax increases, e.g. GST, sales tax. • Subsidy removed by government. • Tax on imports (tariffs) imposed by government. • Price of related good increases – e.g. if the price of adult clothes increases, the firm will make more adult clothes and less kids' clothes.
Subsidy	A payment made by government to firms to keep costs down so supply will increase.
Quota	A restriction on the quantity of imports.
How an overseas trade factor influences supply decisions	A tariff (a tax on imports) imposed by the government will decrease supply in NZ.
How a legal factor might influence the supply decision of a firm	New health and safety standards will increase costs for a firm (as they come up to the new standards) so supply decreases.
How an environmental factor might influence supply decisions of a firm	The use of environment-friendly materials could increase costs to firm so supply will decrease.
A supply curve shift will result in	• a change in the price and quantity supplied of the good. • a change in the output of a related good – e.g. increase in supply of wool will mean reduced output of mutton. • a change in the number of people employed.

Student notes: Supply – Conditions/shifts

QUESTIONS & TASKS

1 a Define the law of supply.

_____

b Explain the difference between an increase in supply and an increase in quantity supplied.

_____

_____

c Give an example of a political factor that could affect supply.

_____

_____

d Write one of the following descriptions for each situation in the table below.

increase in supply   increase in quantity supplied
decrease in supply   decrease in quantity supplied

Situation	Description
(i) costs decrease	
(ii) price increase	
(iii) costs increase	
(iv) price decrease	
(v) new technology	
(vi) a subsidy is removed	
(vii) 	
(viii) an adverse (bad) growing season	
(ix)	

2 **a** Match the graphs below to the situations indicated for the supply of hats – look at the graphs before you start.

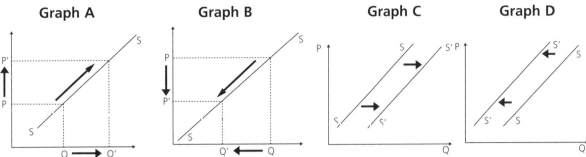

Situation	Graph (either A, B, C, or D)	Situation	Graph (either A, B, C, or D)
A price increase for hats	(i)	A decrease in supply	(viii)
An increase in quantity supplied	(ii)	A fire destroys the hat factory	(ix)
A price decrease for hats	(iii)	A price change for hats	(x)
A decrease in quantity supplied	(iv)	A change in conditions of supply for hats	(xi)
A shift to the right	(v)	Restrictions on importing hats are removed	(xii)
An increase in supply	(vi)	The government gives the hat firm a subsidy to produce hats for school children	(xiii)
A shift to the left	(vii)	Costs of producing hats fall	(xiv)

b What is the cause of a 'shift of' the supply curve? _____

c Explain what is meant by a subsidy.

_____

d Complete the table below by writing in the appropriate answer.

Situation or Graph	Movement or Shift	Choose ONE only of the following: • increase in supply • decrease in supply • increase in quantity supplied • decrease in quantity supplied
(i)		
(ii)		
(iii) costs of production decrease		
(iv) price of product rises		
(v) price of product decreases		
(vi) costs of production increase		
(vii) new technology		
(viii) productivity of workers improves		

3 Carefully label each diagram to show the changes indicated.

a A price increase of 20% from an original price of $50.

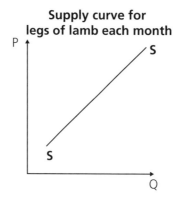

Supply curve for
legs of lamb each month

b A price decrease of 25% from an original price of $120.

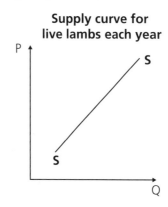

Supply curve for
live lambs each year

c A 50% decrease in the supply of lambs due to a bad lambing season.

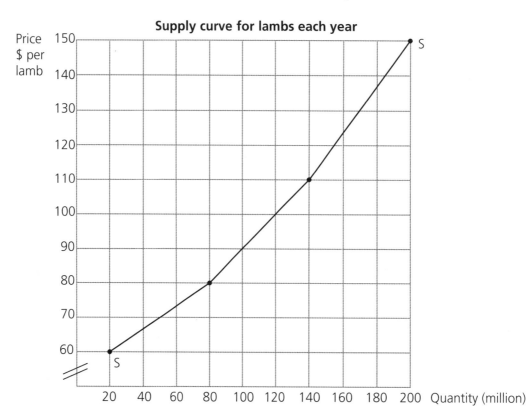

Supply curve for lambs each year

4 a Explain the difference between a change in quantity supplied and a change in supply.

_____

_____

_____

_____

_____

_____

b A bakery can make muffins or cup cakes. Explain the link between a fall in production costs for muffins and the supply of muffins. In your answer refer to how production costs affect supply and one further action that the bakery may take.

_____

_____

_____

_____

_____

_____

_____

_____

_____

_____

c State several reasons for a decrease in supply (a shift of the supply curve to the left).

_____

_____

_____

_____

_____

An increase in supply of onions is not the same
as an increase in quantity supplied of onions.

5 **a** Fully explain the statement above with reference to new technology and price changes. In your answer you should:
- complete the sketch graphs indicated by the title and refer to them in your answer
- explain the reasons for an increase in supply for onions
- explain the reason for an increase in quantity supplied of onions.

An increase in supply for onions

P

S

S

Q

An increase in quantity supplied for onions

P

S

S

Q

----

b Suggest a possible related good for onions and explain why it is a related good.

----

6 Buck Helford Rafting runs white water rafting tours for local and overseas visitors. Consider how each of the following factors would affect Buck's supply.

a Show an increase in supply by 50% for Buck Helford Rafting due to a government subsidy. Label the change fully.

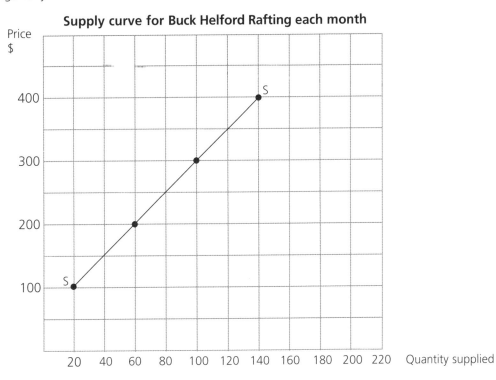

Supply curve for Buck Helford Rafting each month

b New safety regulations are passed requiring rafting operators to provide newly developed safety equipment.

(i) Is this a political, cultural, legal or environmental factor? _____

(ii) Would supply increase or decrease? _____

(iii) Explain why supply would be affected in this way and outline an economic consequence of this change.

_____

_____

_____

c Local iwi have asked the firm to be aware of historical sites along the river bank. Buck has decided to employ local iwi because of their knowledge and understanding of the area.

(i) Is this a political, cultural, legal or environmental factor? _____

(ii) Would supply increase or decrease? _____

(iii) Explain why supply would be affected in this way and outline an economic consequence of this change.

_____

_____

_____

_____

7 Peter is a school student who enjoys brewing his own ginger beer and selling it. At $2 per litre he will produce 50 litres, but if the price doubles he is prepared to supply 200 litres. He would supply 250 litres at $6 per litre and if the price was only $3 per litre he would be prepared to supply 125 litres.

a Use the above information to complete Peter's supply curve for home-brewed ginger beer each month on the grid below.

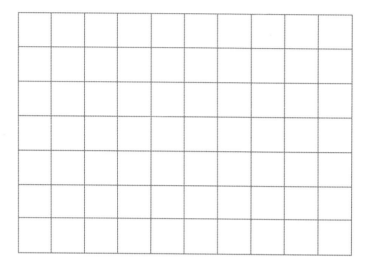

b Suggest a suitable reason why each of the following situations could occur.

(i) Peter chooses to supply 200 litres instead of 50 litres. Assume no change to his supply curve.

_____

_____

(ii) At $3 per litre, Peter chooses to supply 175 litres. _____

_____

(iii) At $6 per litre, Peter chooses to supply 200 litres. _____

_____

_____

(iv) At $1.50 per litre, Peter chooses to produce no ginger beer. _____

_____

_____

c (i) On your graph above, show the effects of a 50% fall in Peter's supply due to an increase in indirect tax.

(ii) Explain the effect an increase in indirect tax will have on the costs of production.

_____

_____

_____

_____

_____

8 Breakthrough Production is a producer of cartoons and promotional videos and DVDs for a range of clients. Their supply is influenced by a number of factors.

a On the supply graphs provided, show the effect that each event below has on the supply of DVDs by using appropriate lines, labels and arrows.

Event 1: Increased wages for workers who produce DVDs
Supply curve for DVDs

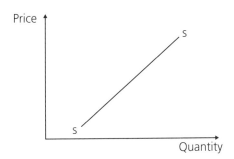

Event 2: Division of labour improves the productivity of DVD workers
Supply curve for DVDs

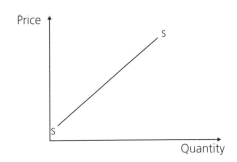

b The graphs below show the effect of other events that have impacted on the supply of DVDs. In the space provided under each graph, identify a specific event (other than Events 1 and 2 above) that would cause the supply change shown.

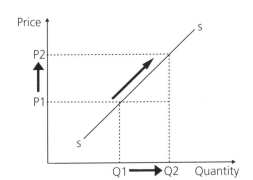

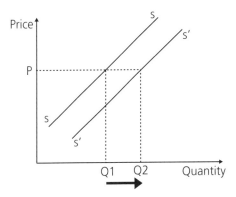

Event (i):

_____

_____

_____

_____

_____

Event (ii):

_____

_____

_____

_____

_____

c State the type of non-economic factor for each situation in the table below.

Situation	Non-economic factor
(i) A business paying to offset carbon emissions.	
(ii) Regulations over product labelling.	
(iii) An increase in quota set by government.	

9 a Use the information in the supply schedule below to complete a supply curve for coffee sold in the café.

Cups of coffee supply schedule each month	
Price ($) per cup	Quantity (cup)
2.00	1 000
2.50	1 700
3.00	2 300
4.00	4 400
4.50	6 000

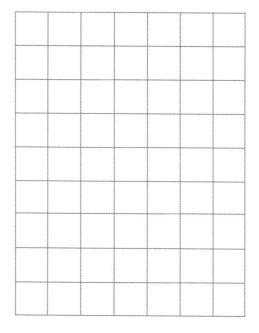

b (i) Use the same axes to illustrate a decrease in price from $4.00 to $3.00.

(ii) Explain the effect on quantity.

_____

c Explain why the café might not increase supply as a result of decreased costs of production.

_____

_____

_____

d Explain how increasing levels of technology are affecting the supply of goods.

_____

_____

_____

e Describe the law of supply.

_____

f What is the only factor that will bring about an increase in quantity supplied?

_____

 ISBN: 9780170415972

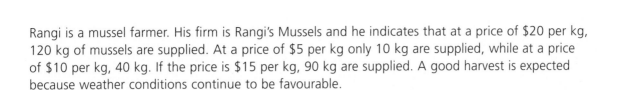

Rangi is a mussel farmer. His firm is Rangi's Mussels and he indicates that at a price of $20 per kg, 120 kg of mussels are supplied. At a price of $5 per kg only 10 kg are supplied, while at a price of $10 per kg, 40 kg. If the price is $15 per kg, 90 kg are supplied. A good harvest is expected because weather conditions continue to be favourable.

10 From the resource material, construct a supply schedule and show the effect of a 50% increase in mussel output while weather conditions continue to be favourable. Discuss the effect the change in weather conditions has on Rangi's supply of mussels. In your answer you should:

- draw a sketch diagram to illustrate the change
- explain the effect this event will have on costs of production
- explain the link between the weather and the supply of mussels and explain a flow-on effect for Rangi's Mussels.

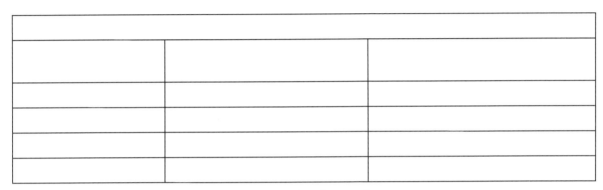

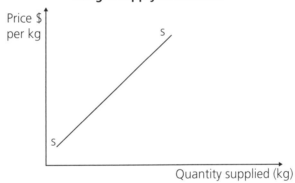

Rangi's supply of mussels

_____
_____
_____
_____
_____
_____
_____
_____
_____
_____
_____
_____
_____

The Surf Warehouse imports surfboards and Stand Up Paddle Boards ((SUPs) from overseas. The government has decided to lower the import tariff on surfboards. Lower import tariffs on surfboards will affect the business of the Surf Warehouse.

11 • On the graph, show the effect of lower import tariffs on the supply of surfboards and stand Up Paddle Boards.

• Explain the effect of lower import tariffs on the supply of surfboards.

• Explain the effect of lower import tariffs on the supply of Stand Up Paddle Boards.

• Explain two consequences that lowering the import tariff will have for the workers at the Surf Warehouse.

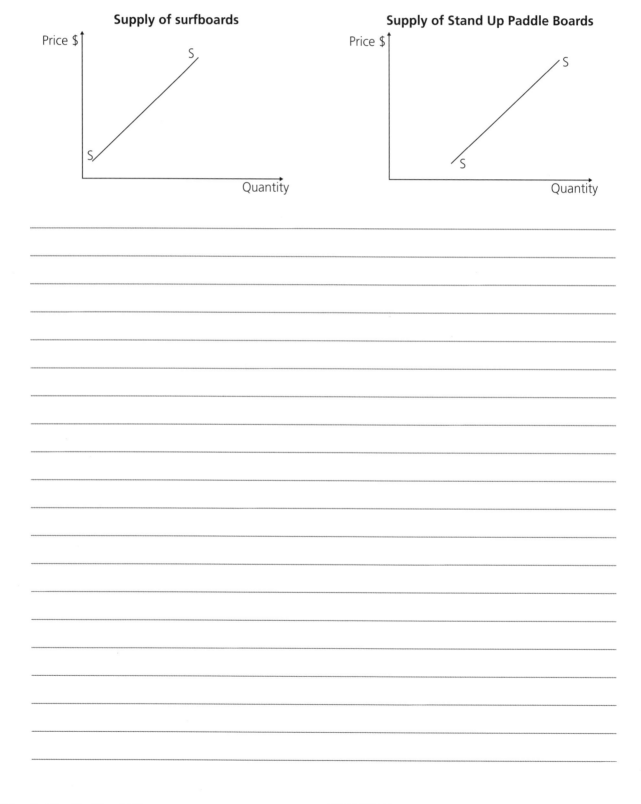

12 a Explain how an increase in a cost of production will affect the supply of a product.

_____

_____

_____

_____

_____

_____

_____

_____

_____

_____

_____

b State several reasons for an increase in supply (a shift of the supply curve to the right).

_____

_____

_____

_____

_____

c Explain why a firm may not increase supply as a result of a decrease in the costs of production.

_____

_____

_____

_____

_____

d Explain the link between stricter health and safety regulations for installing windows, where there is a requirement to have scaffolding signed off by the local council, and costs of production.

_____

_____

_____

_____

Review (exam) questions

Effect of a related good: Kane has a small factory that uses apples from a local orchard to produce apple juice as well as cider.

1 Complete questions **a** and **b** to fully explain the concept of related goods in the context of Kane's business.

   a On the sketch graphs below, show how a decrease in the price of cider might affect Kane's supply of apple juice. Fully label the changes you make on the graphs.

   b Discuss how a decrease in the price of cider will affect Kane's supply of apple juice. In your answer:
   - Explain the relationship between cider and apple juice and how this could affect Kane's use of resources and supply of apple juice.
   - Explain a flow-on effect on Kane's business.

Kane's weekly supply curve for cider

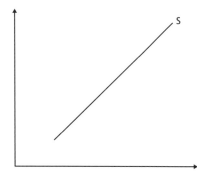

Kane's weekly supply curve for apple juice

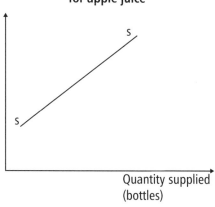

_____

_____

_____

_____

_____

_____

_____

_____

_____

_____

_____

_____

_____

_____

_____

_____

_____

_____

_____

_____

ISBN: 9780170415972

Faster internet is expected to assist firms running their businesses. Ripley's Orchard expects productivity to improve.

2 Explain the effect of new technology on supply in the context of Ripley's Orchard.

  a On the graph below, show how new technology might affect Ripley's Orchard's supply. Fully label the changes.

  b Discuss how this technology might affect the supply of fruit at Ripley's Orchard. In your answer you should:

  • explain the link between technology, productivity and supply

  • refer to the sketch

Ripley's Orchard supply of fruit

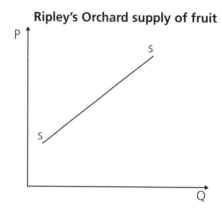

_____

_____

_____

_____

_____

_____

_____

_____

_____

_____

_____

_____

_____

_____

_____

_____

_____

_____

_____

_____

_____

_____

_____

Compliance Costs

When government passes new laws or imposes a new rule or regulation affecting business, the costs to businesses of adopting or responding to the change are known as compliance costs. There can be monetary or time costs in doing PAYE returns, obtaining resource consents or filling in forms for Statistics New Zealand.

Explain the effect of a legal factor on supply in the context of Ripley's Orchard.

c On the sketch graph below, show how a legal factor might affect Ripley's Orchard's supply of fruit. Fully label your changes.

d Explain several consequences of an increase in compliance costs to the owners of Ripley's Orchard. Justify your answer.

Ripley's Orchard supply of fruit

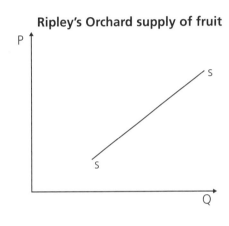

During the winter months Mark runs ski tours. The outlook for the next season is long, cold days.

3 a On the graph, show how the weather is likely to affect Mark's supply of ski tours. Label your graph fully.

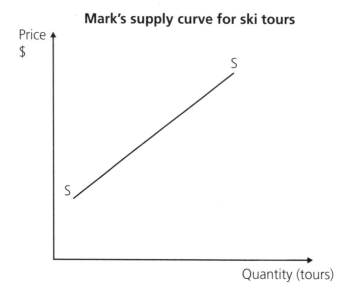

Mark's supply curve for ski tours

b Discuss how the weather is likely to affect Mark's supply of ski tours.

- Explain the link between the weather outlook, profitability and the supply of ski tours. Refer to your supply curve.
- Explain several flow-on effects of this change.

_____

_____

_____

_____

_____

_____

_____

_____

_____

_____

_____

_____

_____

_____

_____

_____

_____

_____

_____

_____

8 MARKET EQUILIBRIUM
Markets, market demand and market supply

The diverse nature of markets

A market is any place or situation where buyers and sellers interact to exchange goods and services. Examples of a place could include retail store, roadside stall, auction or fleamarket. Examples of a 'situation' include mail order, internet website, and telemarketing.

Price is decided in a market in a number of different ways. Price can be set by the seller, set by the government, through bids, tender, auction or by negotiation between the buyer and seller.

Buyers and sellers can communicate in a market in a number of ways ranging from face-to-face (verbal) communication, e-mail, fax, phone or letter.

Market demand

Market demand is the horizontal sum of all individual demand curves and/or schedules at each price. When deriving (calculating) market demand add up the quantity demanded from the individual demand curve, demand schedules or the information given at each price.

	Consumer A	Consumer B	Market Demand
Price $ per kg	Quantity demanded (kgs)	Quantity demanded (kgs)	(Consumer A + Consumer B) (kgs)
5	10	12	22
10	8	9	17
20	4	5	9

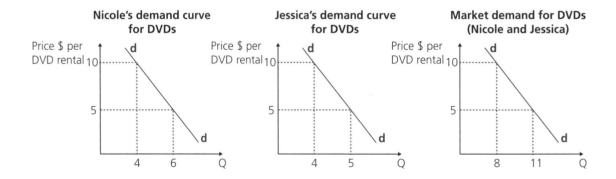

Market supply

Market supply is the horizontal sum of all firms' supply curves and/or schedules at each price. When deriving (calculating) market supply add up the quantity supplied from the firms' supply curves, supply schedules or the information given at each price.

Price $ per kg	Firm A Quantity supplied (kgs)	Firm B Quantity supplied (kgs)	Market supply (Firm A + Firm B) (kgs)
5	4	5	9
10	8	9	17
20	12	11	23

Producer C supply curve

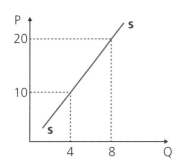

Producer D supply curve

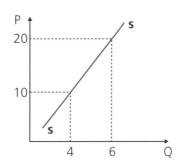

Market supply (Producer C and Producer D)

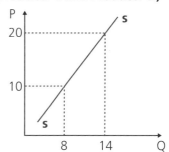

Key terms and ideas

Market	Place (or situation) where buyers and sellers exchange goods and services. A market occurs whenever sellers and buyers interact to exchange goods and services.
Examples of markets	auction roadside stall Internet shopping site retail shop fair garage sale private sale fleamarket Stock Exchange telemarketing tender
How price is decided in a market	Set by the seller, set by the government, through bids, tender, auction or by negotiation.
How buyers and sellers communicate in a market	Face-to-face (verbal), e-mail, internet, fax, phone or letter.
Market supply	• Total of *all* firms' supply curves/schedules at each price. • Horizontal sum of *all* firms' supply curves/schedules at each price. e.g. FIRM A + FIRM B = MARKET SUPPLY
Market demand	• Total of everyone's individual demand curves/schedules at each price. • Horizontal sum of all individual demand curves/schedules at each price. **Don't** add in the price to work out market demand; in this case market demand is adding up the quantity demanded by the three individuals at each price.

Price $	Saskia's quantity demanded	Sam's quantity demanded	Harry's quantity demanded	Market demand
10	6	7	3	16
20	4	5	1	10

    ISBN: 9780170415972

Student notes: Market equilibrium – Markets, market demand and market supply

Price ($)	Consumer X quantity demanded	Consumer Y quantity demanded	Consumer Z quantity demanded	Market quantity demanded
1	7	8		24
2	6	6		19
3	5	4	5	
4	4	2	3	

Market demand curve for a particular product

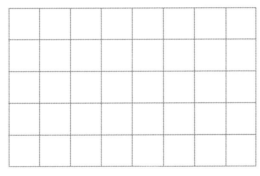

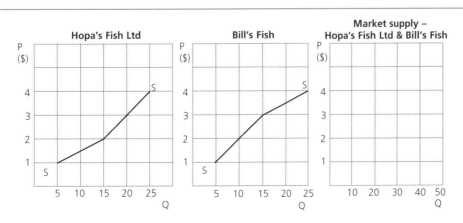

Hopa's Fish Ltd

Bill's Fish

Market supply – Hopa's Fish Ltd & Bill's Fish

1 Rob, Bernie and Mike are always losing golf balls and often have to buy more. Shown below are the individual demand details for golf balls for Rob, Bernie and Mike.

Rob's demand schedule for golf balls	
Price ($)	Quantity demanded
2.50	10
5.00	5
7.50	2

Bernie's demand schedule for golf balls	
Price ($)	Quantity demanded
2.50	8
5.00	6
7.50	3

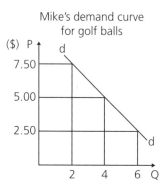

Mike's demand curve for golf balls

a Explain how the market demand curve is derived.

_____

_____

_____

b In the table below, complete the market demand schedule for golf balls from the information above. Assume that Rob, Bernie and Mike are the only three buyers of golf balls.

2 a Draw the market curve for ice-blocks using the tables below.

Sandra's demand for ice-blocks	
Price ($)	Ice-blocks
0.50	14
1.00	9
1.50	5

Stefan's demand for ice-blocks	
Price ($)	Ice-blocks
0.50	16
1.00	9
1.50	7

Market demand curve for ice-blocks

Betty's demand for ice-blocks	
Price ($)	Ice-blocks
0.50	15
1.00	9
1.50	6

b Clearly show on the graph the effect of a price change from $1.00 to $0.50 on the curve you have drawn.

     ISBN: 9780170415972

3 a Calculate the missing quantity supplied, then write the correct figures in the spaces in the schedule below.

Market supply for pizza				
Price ($)	Quantity supplied (A)	Quantity supplied (B)	Quantity supplied (C)	Market supply
2	0	20		75
4	30		75	150
6	50	75	100	
8		90	130	300

b Define market supply.

_____

_____

_____

_____

c Calculate the missing quantity demanded, then write the correct figures in the spaces in the schedule below.

Market demand for pizza				
Price ($)	Quantity demanded (A)	Quantity demanded (B)	Quantity demanded (C)	Market demand
8		75	50	175
6	60	100		225
4	80		75	275
2	105	130	90	

d Define market demand.

_____

_____

_____

_____

4 **a** The tables below show the quantity supplied by three firms who make ice cream. Graph the MARKET SUPPLY from this information on the grid below.

Riley's	
Price ($ per litre)	Quantity supplied (litres)
1	0
2	7
3	10

Allot's	
Price ($ per litre)	Quantity supplied (litres)
1	1
2	8
3	15

Young's	
Price ($ per litre)	Quantity supplied (litres)
1	2
2	12
3	14

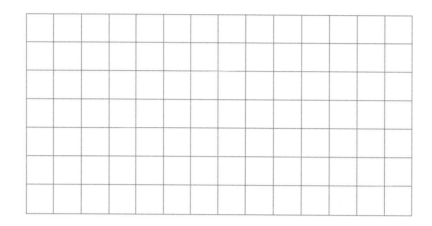

b On the graph you have drawn, show the effect of a tighter standards regulation for ice cream production.

c Explain why the market supply would react in the way you showed in your answer to question **b**.

_____

d Suggest a reason why the supply of ice cream from Riley's is zero at $1.

_____

e Explain how the quantities for a market supply curve are calculated.

_____

_____

5 **a** What is a quota? How does a quota on New Zealand coal to Europe affect New Zealand coal production?

Quota: _____

Effect on New Zealand coal production: _____

There are three firms able to supply coal to the market. Huntly Coal is prepared to supply 400 tonnes of coal at $200 per tonne, 800 tonnes at $400 per tonne and 500 tonnes at $300 per tonne. Norwest Coal is prepared to supply 100 tonnes of coal less than Huntly coal at each price. South Coal is prepared to supply 100 tonnes of coal at $200 per tonne, 300 tonnes at $300 per tonne and 400 tonnes at $400 per tonne.

b Complete the following supply schedule based on the information above.

Price ($ per tonne)	Huntly Coal Quantity supplied (tonnes)	Norwest Coal Quantity supplied (tonnes)	South Coal Quantity supplied (tonnes)	Market Quantity supplied (tonnes)

6 The local school uses its gym and tennis courts each Friday night as a venue where local crafts people set up stalls to sell their goods and services.

a Define the term market.

_____

b Describe how the school gym and tennis courts fits the definition of a market.

_____

_____

c At the school fleamarket there is a variety of organic apples supplied in the market. Explain how market supply is derived, i.e., calculated.

_____

_____

d Describe how buyers and sellers communicate in this market.

_____

e State the most likely way price would be decided in this market.

_____

f Buyers and sellers communicate in the market in various ways. For each example given in the table below describe how the communication took place.

Example	Communication type
A supplier confirms an order with a client using the internet.	
A student goes door to door selling pizza deals from a local firm.	
An exact copy of a document is sent electronically along a telephone line requesting books from a supplier that the local book store will resell to its customers.	
A piece of writing addressed to a mail order firm sent through the postal service.	

g Price can be decided in the market in various ways. Complete the table below by describing the ways in which price is decided in each situation.

Situation	The way price is decided in this market
(i) A house is sold to the person who offers to pay the highest price on the day by a series of bids.	
(ii) A firm makes a formal (written) offer to supply goods or do a job for a particular price for a client.	
(iii) Sam offers to pay $200 for a secondhand surfboard at a garage sale.	
(iv) Parliament determines that the maximum price of bread is $2.00 per loaf.	
(v) The price of food for sale in the school tuckshop is set by the owner.	
(vi) A Barry Crump book is sold on a Trade Me internet site.	

Review (exam) questions

1 Assume the individual demand data in the table below is the total of all demand for beef sold at this shop each month.
- On the grid below draw the market demand curve for beef in this very small market.
- Show on your graph the effects of a change in price from $5 to $12 per kilogram.
- Explain the difference between individual demand and market demand.

Monthly demand for beef			
Price ($ per kg)	Ameer's quantity demanded (kg)	Lucy's quantity demanded (kg)	Gavin's quantity demanded (kg)
5	20	60	40
10	10	40	30
15	10	20	30
20	0	10	30
25	0	0	10

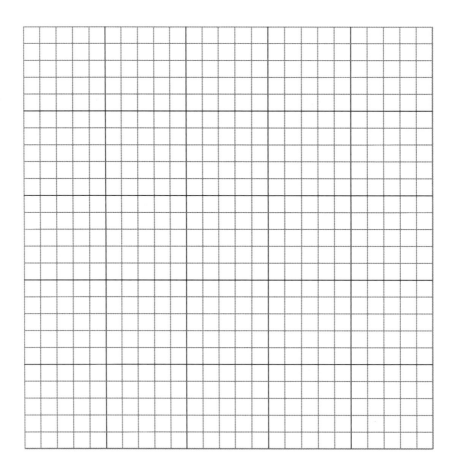

_____

_____

_____

_____

_____

Price ($/kg)	Fred's quantity supplied (kg)	Tua's quantity supplied (kg)	Fish Ltd quantity supplied (kg)
5.00	20	40	40
5.50	30	50	90
6.00	40	60	100
6.50	50	70	110
7.00	60	70	110

2 Draw up a market supply curve for fish given the information above.
   • Show on the graph what would happen if the price increased from $5.50 per kg to $6.50 per kg.
   • Name two factors that will cause a shift of the supply curve for fish to the left.
   • Explain the difference between a decrease in supply and a decrease in quantity supplied.

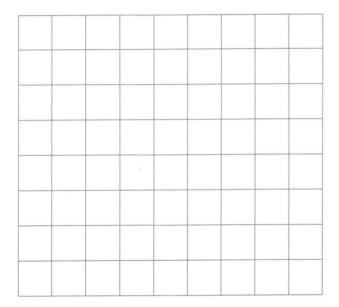

3 Supply is the quantity of a good or service a supplier will be willing to bring to the market at a range of prices. Explain market supply. In your answer you should:
- Explain how a market supply curve is derived.
- Construct a fully labelled and accurate market supply curve from the information provided.

Supply Schedule for Mussels		
Price ($ per kg)	Quantity Supplied North Island (kg)	Quantity Supplied South Island (kg)
10	0	0
30	30 000	50 000
40	60 000	60 000
60	80 000	60 000

_____
_____
_____
_____
_____
_____
_____
_____
_____
_____
_____
_____
_____
_____

       ISBN: 9780170415972

Establishing market equilibrium

Market for Pizza Weekly				
Price $	Quantity Demanded	Quantity Supplied	Market Situation	Pressure on Price
14	0	12000	Surplus 12000	Downward
12	2000	10000	Surplus 8000	Downward
10	4000	8000	Surplus 4000	Downward
8	6000	6000	Equilibrium	None/Stable
6	8000	4000	Shortage 4000	Upward
4	10000	2000	Shortage 8000	Upward
2	12000	0	Shortage 12000	Upward

Equilibrium is a term to denote a balance between forces involved. The **equilibrium price and equilibrium quantity** in a market is determined by the interaction of the forces of demand and supply. Equilibrium in a market is the price at which the quantity demanded by consumers equals the quantity supplied by producers. At the equilibrium, both parties involved in the market are completely satisfied, with consumers having purchased all they want to buy, and producers having sold all they want to sell.

At the market equilibrium the **market will clear** and there will be neither a surplus (excess supply) or a shortage (excess demand). Therefore, all stock is sold (i.e., no stock is unsold) and consumers do not want to buy any more of the good or service. As long as the conditions of demand and conditions of supply remain unchanged (ceteris paribus) then the equilibrium price and equilibrium quantity will remain unchanged.

On a schedule the equilibrium can be found where the quantity demanded by consumers and the quantity supplied by producers are equal at one particular price.

On the diagram, the equilibrium price for pizza is $8 (Pe) and the equilibrium

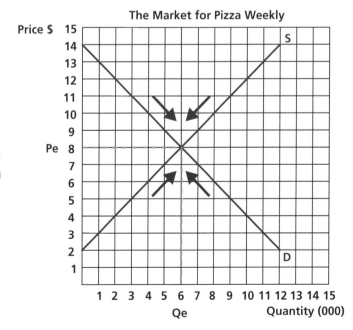

The Market for Pizza Weekly

quantity for pizza is 6 000 (Qe) because this is where the demand curve and the supply curve intersect, with the quantity demanded by consumers equal to the quantity supplied by firms.

Shortage (excess demand)

A **shortage (excess demand)** will occur at any price below the equilibrium where the quantity supplied by producers is less than the quantity demanded by consumers. When there is a shortage the market will react with consumers bidding up the price. As the price of a good or service increases quantity supplied increases because selling the good or providing that service becomes relatively more profitable for firms because the revenue (income) they earn is higher and firms will be more able to cover costs. As the price of a good or service increases consumers' real incomes fall and the good or service becomes relatively less affordable, consumers will be less willing and able to purchase the good or service with their limited incomes and look to buy more of a relatively cheaper substitute.

A shortage of 8 000 will occur at $4 (P1) because at this price the quantity supplied by producers (Qs, 2 000) is less than the quantity demanded by consumers (Qd, 10 000). As price increases the quantity demanded by consumers decreases from 10 000 (Qd) to 6 000 (Qe), while the quantity supplied by producers increases from 2 000 (Qs) to 6 000 (Qe). Equilibrium is restored at $8 (Pe) where quantity supplied equals quantity demanded of 6 000 (Qe) and the market clears.

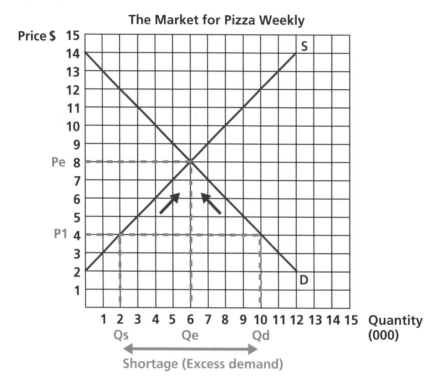

At any price below the equilibrium the quantity sold in the market equals the quantity supplied by producers. There is no unsold stock at any price below the equilibrium.

Surplus (excess supply)

A **surplus (excess supply)** will occur at any price above the equilibrium where the quantity supplied by producers is greater than the quantity demanded by consumers. When there is a surplus the market will react with firms willing to accept a lower price to get rid of unsold stock. As the price of a good or service decreases quantity supplied decreases because selling the good or providing that service becomes relatively less profitable for firms because the revenue (income) they earn is lower and firms will be less able to cover costs. As the price of a good or service decreases consumers' real incomes rise and the good or service becomes relatively more affordable, consumers will be more willing and able to purchase the good or service with their limited incomes and look to buy less of a relatively more expensive substitute.

A surplus of 4 000 will occur at $10 (P2) because at this price the quantity supplied by producers (Qs, 8 000) is greater than the quantity demanded by consumers (Qd, 4 000). As the price decreases the quantity demanded by consumers increases from 4 000 (Qd) to 6000 (Qe), while the quantity supplied by producers decreases from 8 000 (Qs) to 6 000 (Qs). Equilibrium is restored at $8 (Pe) where quantity supplied equals quantity demanded of 6 000 (Qe) and the market clears.

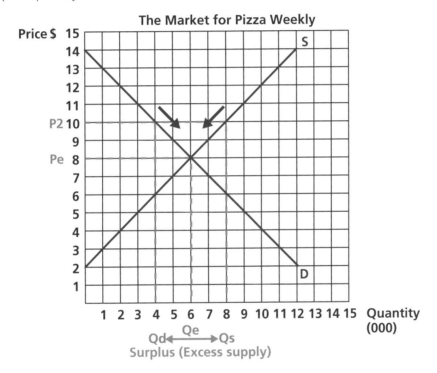

At any price above the equilibrium the quantity sold in the market equals the quantity demanded by consumers. The quantity of the stock unsold in the market equals the size of the surplus.

Key terms and ideas

Equilibrium	
	• The price at which quantity demanded equals quantity supplied. • The position where there is no tendency to change and where the market tends to move towards. • The price at which there is neither a surplus nor shortage, and the market clears.
Shortage (excess demand) is the size of the gap between the demand and supply curves below the equilibrium	
Surplus (excess supply) is the size of the gap between the demand and supply curves above the equilibrium	
How will the market react to a shortage (excess demand)? Explain why a shortage will not last long in the market	Market forces return it to the equilibrium as consumers bid the price up so the quantity supplied will increase and quantity demanded falls.
How will the market react to a surplus (excess supply)? Explain why a surplus will not last long in the market	Market forces return it to the equilibrium. Firms will accept lower prices so the quantity supplied falls and the quantity demanded increases.

Student notes: Market equilibrium – Basics

ISBN: 9780170415972

QUESTIONS & TASKS

1 Draw up the market for pizza per month using the schedules below.

Price ($)	Market demand	Market supply
3	300	80
5	220	180
6	180	240
8	140	280
12	100	320

a What is the equilibrium price and quantity for a pizza?

price = _____   quantity = _____

b Explain what is meant by the term 'a market'.

_____

_____

c **(i)** On your graph, show the market situation if the price of a pizza was $8. Fully label the graph.

   (ii) Explain why the price of a pizza is likely to fall in this situation.

_____

_____

2 a Use the schedules below for Trans-Tasman Airline Flights (one way) each month. Clearly label all parts and use dotted lines to indicate the market equilibrium as Pe and Qe.

Price ($)	Market demand (000)	Market supply (000)
750	10	150
500	40	130
400	50	110
300	80	80
100	140	10

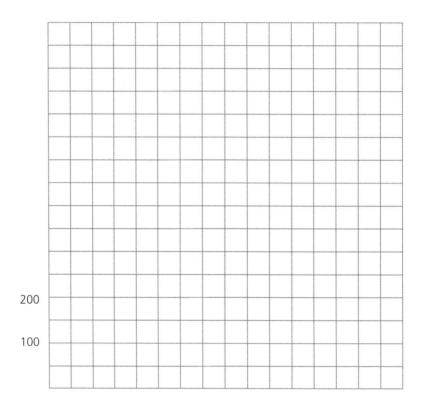

b What is the equilibrium price and quantity?   price = _____   quantity = _____

c Using dotted lines, show and label any resulting **surplus** or **shortage** when the price is $150.

d Explain how the market would react to this situation and how equilibrium would be restored. Refer to both price and quantity.

_____

_____

_____

_____

_____

_____

_____

3 At a price of $6.00, the market supply of DVD movies each week is 250. As the price falls to $5.00 the quantity supplied falls by 20%. If the price is $2.00 the supply is 100 and 120 at $3.00.

a Draw the market for DVD movie rentals each week from the information provided.

Price ($)	Market demand
6.00	100
5.00	120
3.00	200
2.00	250

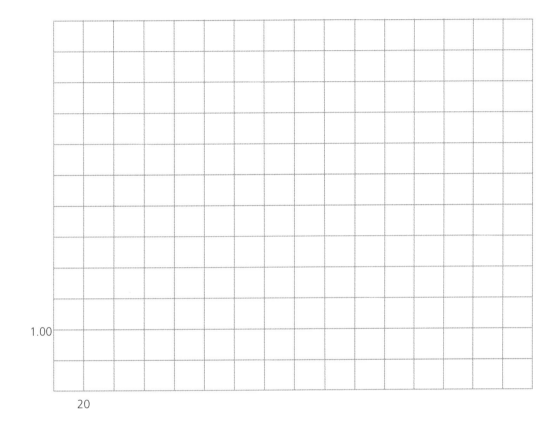

1.00

20

b Identify the equilibrium price and quantity.   price = _____   quantity = _____

c **(i)** On your graph, show the market situation if the price of a DVD movie rental was $3.00. Fully label the graph.

(ii) Explain why the price of a DVD is likely to rise in this situation.

_____

(iii) Explain fully how the equilibrium quantity is restored when the price increases. Use the terms 'quantity supplied' and 'quantity demanded' in your answer.

_____

_____

_____

_____

_____

4 At $40 a life jacket the market demand was 12 000. As price increased by 50% the market demand fell 25%. If the price was $80 market demand would be 6 000. At $140 the market was 2 000 and if the price was $100 then demand was 4 000.

a Plot the market for lifejackets each year in the grid below, using the information provided.

Lifejacket market	
Price ($)	Market supply
40	1 000
60	3 000
80	6 000
100	8 000
140	11 000

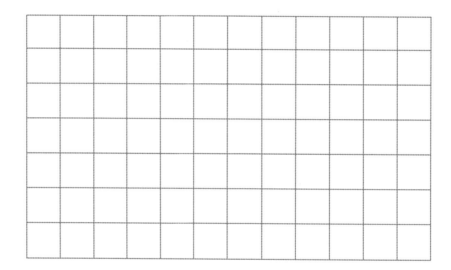

b **(i)** Identify the equilibrium price and quantity. price = _____ quantity = _____

  (ii) Label the equilibrium price (P1) and quantity (Q1).

c At what price is there a surplus of 4 000? _____

d How will the market react to a surplus?

_____

_____

_____

_____

e **(i)** Markets are diverse in a number of ways. State TWO different ways price could be decided in a market.

_____

  (ii) State TWO different ways sellers and buyers could communicate with each other in a market.

_____

5 Study the graph and answer the questions that follow.

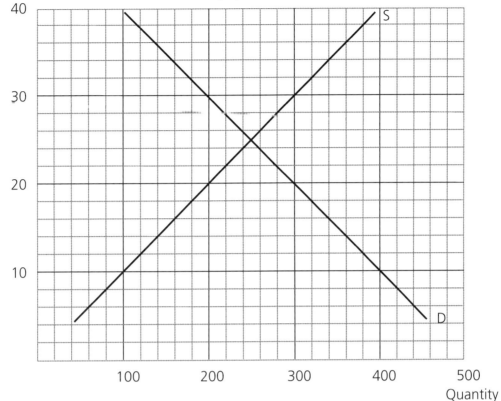

Market for paperback books each week

a Identify the price where there is:

    (i) neither a shortage nor surplus _____

    (ii) a shortage of 60 _____

    (iii) a shortage of 220 _____

    (iv) a shortage of 300 _____

    (v) a surplus of 100 _____

    (vi) a surplus of 260 _____

b Why would a shortage not last long in the market?

_____

_____

_____

_____

_____

_____

_____

c How many paperback books will be sold at the following prices?

    (i) $30 _____

    (ii) $20 _____

    (iii) $10 _____

    (iv) $40 _____

6 Use the graph below to answer the questions that follow.

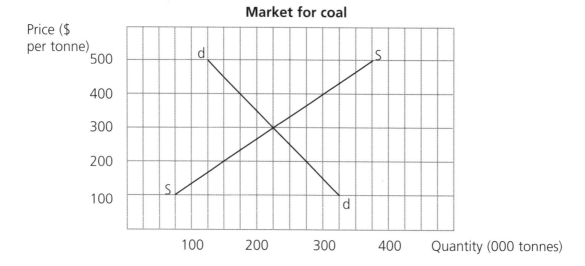

Market for coal

Price ($ per tonne) vs Quantity (000 tonnes)

a Complete the table below for coal.

Price $ per tonne	Market demand (000 tonnes)	Market supply (000 tonnes)
500		
		225
200		
	325	

b **(i)** Name the price where neither a shortage nor surplus will occur. _____

(ii) On the graph and using dotted lines, identify and label clearly the following:

- equilibrium quantity (label **Qe**)
- equilibrium price (label **Pe**).

c **(i)** On the graph above, show the market situation if the price of coal was $500 per tonne. Use dotted lines to show the quantity demanded (Qd) and quantity supplied (Qs). Label the resulting **shortage** or **surplus**.

(ii) Fully explain how the market will react to a price of $500 per tonne.

_____

_____

_____

_____

_____

_____

_____

_____

_____

_____

7 Study the graph and answer the questions that follow.

a Work out the missing quantity supplied and write them in the space provided.

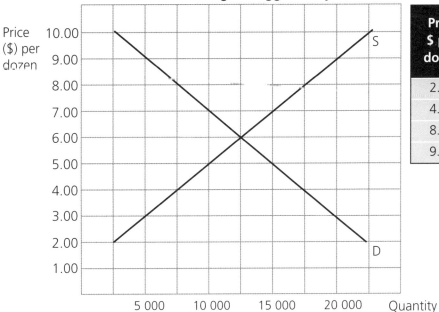

Market for organic eggs each year

Price $ per dozen	Fresh eggs Quantity supplied	Natures Ways Quantity supplied
2.00	1 000	
4.00	3 250	
8.00		11 000
9.00		12 000

b What is the equilibrium price and quantity?

Price _____ Quantity _____

c Identify the price where a surplus of 5 000 will occur. Also identify at this price the quantity demanded and the quantity supplied.

Price _____ Quantity demanded _____ Quantity supplied _____

d How will the market react to a surplus of 5 000?

_____

_____

_____

_____

e Explain how the quantities for a market supply curve are derived.

_____

_____

f Explain why firms supply more as the price increases.

_____

_____

Review (exam) questions

Lou conducts a survey about the firms that produce snowboards. The results are given below.

Monthly supply schedule for snowboards				
Price $	Rave Boards	Just Boards	Boards R Us	Market quantity supplied
200	25	75	150	
600	200	600		1 500
1 000		1 200	1 300	3 000
1 400	600		1 400	3 500

1 **a** Calculate the missing quantity supplied, then write the correct figures in the spaces in the schedule above.

b **(i)** On the grid below plot the Monthly Supply Curve for Snowboards. Label the Market Supply MS.

(ii) On the graph and using dotted lines identify and label clearly the equilibrium price (Pe) and equilibrium quantity (Qe).

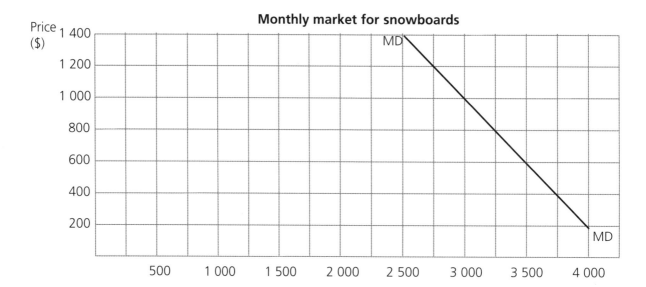

PHOTOCOPYING OF THIS PAGE IS RESTRICTED UNDER LAW.   ISBN: 9780170415972

c Using data from the graph on the previous page, fully explain how the market will restore equilibrium when there is a surplus. In your answer:

- describe what a surplus is

- identify a price where there is a surplus

- explain the producers' reaction

- use the law of supply and the law of demand.

_____

_____

_____

_____

_____

_____

_____

_____

_____

_____

_____

_____

_____

_____

_____

_____

_____

_____

_____

_____

_____

_____

_____

_____

_____

_____

_____

Information from consumers about the milk they purchased at several supermarkets was collated in the table below.

Weekly demand schedule for milk				
Price $ per 2-litre container	Supermarket Plus	Supermarket Warehouse	Supermarket Store	Market quantity demanded
1.50	7 000		15 000	30 000
2.50		5 000	9 000	20 000
3.50	4 000	3 000		15 000
4.50	1 000	500	3 500	

2 **a** Work out the missing values for the quantity demanded at the various prices, than write the correct answer in the missing space in the table above.

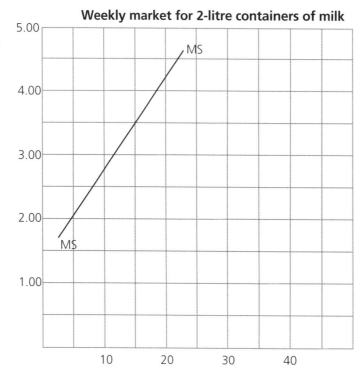

Weekly market for 2-litre containers of milk

b (i) On the grid above plot the Weekly Market Demand Curve for 2-litre Containers of Milk. Label the Market Demand MD.

(ii) On the graph and using dotted lines identify and label clearly the equilibrium price (Pe) and equilibrium quantity (Qe).

     ISBN: 9780170415972

c Using data from the graph on the previous page, fully explain how the market will restore equilibrium when there is a shortage. In your answer:

- describe what a shortage is
- identify a price where there is a shortage
- explain the consumers' reaction
- use the law of supply and the law of demand.

_____

_____

_____

_____

_____

_____

_____

_____

_____

_____

_____

_____

_____

_____

_____

_____

_____

_____

_____

_____

_____

_____

_____

_____

_____

_____

_____

_____

_____

The table illustrates the market for business class flights between Auckland and Sydney.

Weekly market for business class flights (return) between Auckland and Sydney		
Price ($)	Market supply	Market demand
2 000	8 000	1 000
1 500	7 000	2 000
1 000	4 500	4 500
500	2 000	7 000

3 **a** Use the schedule to draw the graph of business class flights between Auckland and Sydney (return) in the grid below. Indicate the market equilibrium price (Pe) and quantity (Qe).

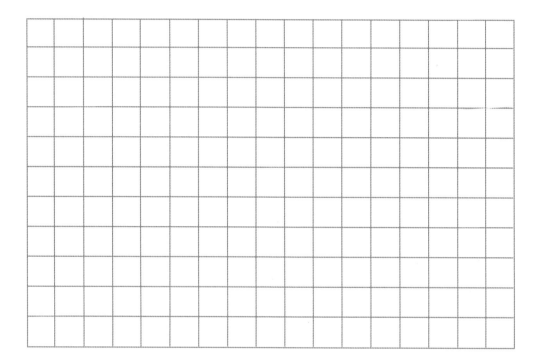

b On the graph you drew above, show the market situation if the price of a business class return flight between Auckland and Sydney was $800. You must use dotted lines to show the quantity demanded (label this Qd) and the quantity supplied (label this Qs). Label the resulting shortage or surplus.

c Discuss how the market would react to this situation. In your answer you should explain the change in the market price, the change in quantity demanded and quantity supplied. Refer to the data given.

_____

_____

_____

_____

_____

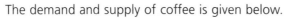

The demand and supply of coffee is given below.

At $3 a cup the market demand is 1 000 per day. At $4 individuals buy 800.

At $5 market demand is 400, while at $6 consumers purchase 200 cups.

Market supply schedule for coffee daily	
Price $	Market supply
6	1 100
5	700
4	500
3	200

4 **a** On the graph below plot the market for coffee daily. Use dotted lines to show the market equilibrium price (P1) and quantity (Q1).

b On the graph you drew above, show the market situation if the price of a cup of coffee was $5.00. You must use dotted lines to show the quantity demanded (label this Qd) and the quantity supplied (label this Qs). Label the resulting shortage or surplus.

c Discuss how the market would react to this situation. In your answer you should explain the change in the market price, the change in quantity demanded and quantity supplied. Refer to the data given.

_____

_____

_____

_____

A new equilibrium

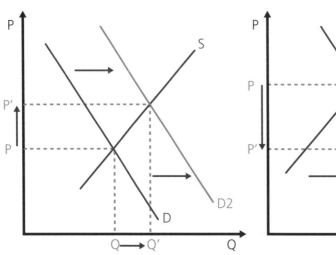

An increase in demand when the demand curve shifts to the right and both equilibrium price and quantity will increase.

An increase in supply when the supply curve shifts to the right and equilibrium price will decrease and quantity increase.

When ceteris paribus is broken and the conditions of demand or supply change then there will be a new equilibrium price and equilibrium quantity as one or both curves (demand and supply) shift.

To illustrate a change in the market due to a shift of a curve, these conventions are followed:

The new demand and/or supply curves are drawn parallel to the original curves, with appropriate labels for the new curves including direction arrows.

The new equilibrium price is labelled P′ or P2 and the new equilibrium quantity is labelled Q′ or Q2.

Direction arrows are used to show the increase or decrease in price and/or quantity that result in the market. Two possible outcomes are shown above.

When the demand and/or supply curves shift there is likely to be a shortage or surplus at the original equilibrium price.

An increase in supply or a decrease in demand will result in a surplus existing at the original equilibrium price. If the shift creates an excess supply (surplus) at the original equilibrium price then the market will react and the equilibrium price will fall.

A decrease in supply or an increase in demand will result in a shortage existing at the original equilibrium price. If the shift creates an excess demand (shortage) at the original equilibrium price then the market will react and the equilibrium price will rise.

Shortage (excess demand) and shifts of the demand and/or supply curves

A shortage (excess demand) will occur where the quantity supplied by producers is less than the quantity demanded by consumers. When the condition of ceteris paribus is relaxed and there is either an increase in demand (an outward shift of the demand curve) and/or a decrease in supply (an inward shift of the supply curve), this will create a shortage (excess demand) at the original price.

The market will react to a shortage with consumers bidding up the price. Price rises, until equilibrium price and quantity is reached and the market clears.

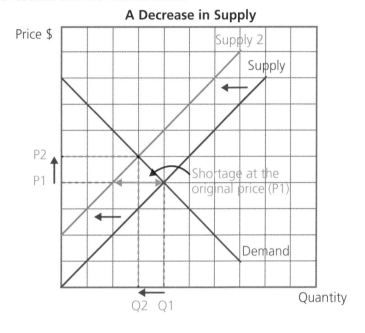

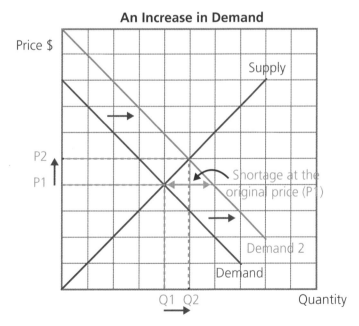

Surplus (excess supply) and shifts of the demand and/or supply curve

A surplus (excess supply) will occur where the quantity supplied by producers is greater than the quantity demanded by consumers.

When the condition of ceteris paribus is relaxed and there is either a decrease in demand (an inward shift of the demand curve) and/or an increase in supply (an outward shift of the supply curve), this will create a surplus (excess supply) at the original price.

When there is a surplus, firms will accept a lower price to get rid of unsold stock. The price falls, until the equilibrium price and quantity is reached and the market clears.

An Increase in Supply

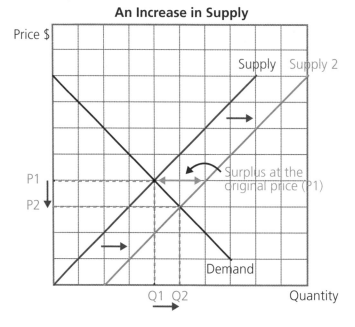

A Decrease in Demand

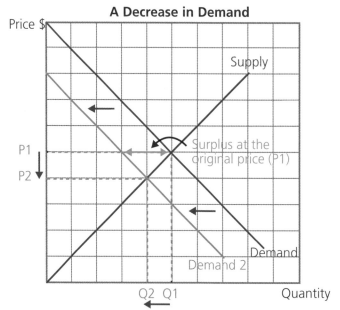

PHOTOCOPYING OF THIS PAGE IS RESTRICTED UNDER LAW.   ISBN: 9780170415972

Key terms and ideas

Labelling a graph after a change in conditions of demand or supply	Label the original equilibrium price (Pe, P1) and quantity (Qe, Q1). Label the new equilibrium price (Pe1, P2) and quantity (Qe1, Q2). Indicate the increase or decrease in the price and quantity by using direction arrows.
A surplus at the original equilibrium price …	Occurs when there is either an increase in supply or a decrease in demand. The market will react and the price will fall. **A Decrease in Demand**
A shortage at the original equilibrium price …	Occurs when there is either a decrease in supply or an increase in demand. The market will react and the price will rise. **A Decrease in Supply**

Student notes: Market equilibrium – Price & output changes

ISBN: 9780170415972

QUESTIONS & TASKS

1 **a** Draw the change indicated by the TITLE of each graph and label each diagram fully. Label the original price and quantity as P and Q respectively. Label the new price and quantity as P' and Q' respectively.

(i)   **A decrease in supply**

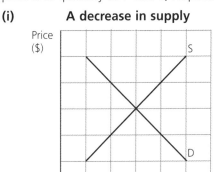

(ii)   **An increase in supply**

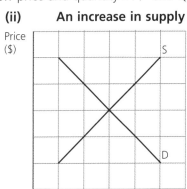

(iii)   **An increase in demand**

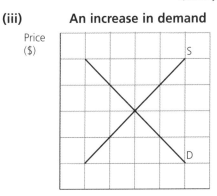

(iv)   **A decrease in demand**

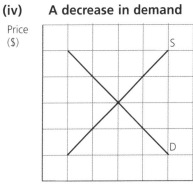

b Conditions or determinants of demand and supply. Write 'demand' or 'supply' for each idea below depending on what condition each statement represents. The first one is done for you.

(i)	income is a condition of	demand	**(ix)**	price of a substitute is a condition of	
(ii)	sales tax is a condition of		**(x)**	price of a complement is a condition of	
(iii)	subsidy is a condition of		**(xi)**	GST is a condition of	
(iv)	tariff is a condition of		**(xii)**	indirect tax is a condition of	
(v)	advertising is a condition of		**(xiii)**	direct tax is a condition of	
(vi)	cost of raw materials is a condition of		**(xiv)**	productivity is a condition of	
(vii)	technology is a condition of		**(xv)**	flood, strike, disease is a condition of	
(viii)	fashion/taste is a condition of		**(xvi)**	price of a related good is a condition of	

2 a Students are encouraged to bring their own laptops, smartphones or tablets to use in schools. Show the change this has had on the market for smartphones. Label the new equilibrium price and quantity as P1 and Q1 respectively.

New Zealand market for smartphones

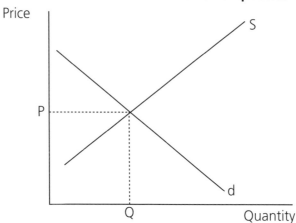

b (i) State the situation that would exist in the market if the price remained at the original equilibrium P.

_____

(ii) Explain the market forces that result in the new equilibrium price and quantity, at P1 and Q1.

_____

_____

_____

_____

_____

_____

_____

_____

_____

_____

c Complete these statements.

(i) A decrease in demand will create a _____ at the original equilibrium price.

(ii) An increase in demand will create a _____ at the original equilibrium price.

(iii) A decrease in supply will create a _____ at the original equilibrium price.

(iv) An increase in supply will create a _____ at the original equilibrium price.

 ISBN: 9780170415972

3 **a** The number of liquor store operators has increased over recent years. Draw and label a new market supply
curve to show this effect. Label the new equilibrium price and quantity, P1 and Q1 respectively.

Market for alcohol in New Zealand

b **(i)** State the situation that would exist in the market if price remained at the original equilibrium
Pe.

_____

(ii) Explain the market forces that result in the new equilibrium price and quantity, at P1 and Q1.

_____

_____

_____

_____

c Complete these statements.

(i) If there is an _____ or a _____

_____ it will create a surplus at the original equilibrium price.

(ii) If there is a _____ or an _____

_____ it will create a shortage at the original equilibrium price.

d Complete the table.

Possible cause of a price rise in the market for alcohol in New Zealand	
Demand factor	Supply factor

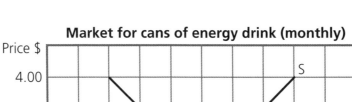

Market for cans of energy drink (monthly)

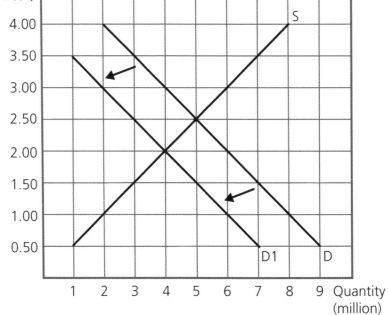

4 a On the graph above label:
- the original equilibrium price (Pe) and quantity (Qe)
- the new equilibrium price (Pe2) and quantity (Qe2)
- label the resulting shortage/surplus at the original equilibrium.

b (i) Use the graph to complete the table.

	Original equilibrium	New equilibrium
Price		
Quantity		
Producer revenue (show working)		

(ii) Explain the change in revenue received by producers. Refer to the graph.

_____

_____

_____

_____

A major storm has damaged strawberry crops and other agricultural produce.

Market for strawberries (annually)

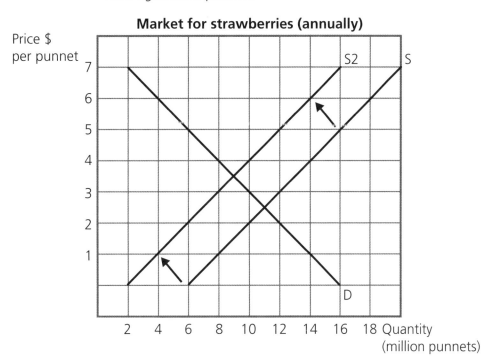

Price $ per punnet

Quantity (million punnets)

5 a On the graph above label:
  - the equilibrium price before the storm (P1) and quantity (Q1)
  - the equilibrium price after the storm (P2) and quantity (Q2)
  - label the resulting shortage/surplus at the original equilibrium.

b (i) Use the graph to complete the table.

	After the storm	Before the storm
Price		
Quantity		
Consumer spending (show working)		

(ii) Explain the change in consumer spending. Refer to the graph.

_____

_____

_____

_____

_____

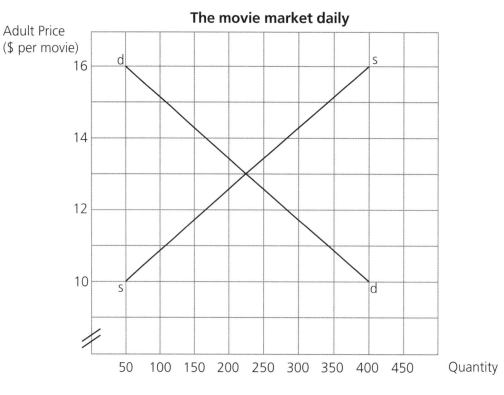

The movie market daily

6 **a** **(i)** From the information contained in the graph above, construct a market demand and market supply schedule in the table below.

The movie market daily		
Adult price ($)	**Market supply**	**Market demand**
10		
12		
14		
16		

(ii) On the graph above, identify the market price as Pe and the market quantity as Qe.

b As a result of increased competition from cheaper DVD rentals, there is a 50% decrease in the number of people going to the movies.

(i) Draw a new market demand curve, labelled Md′.

(ii) Identify the new market price as P1′ and new market quantity as Q1′.

c **(i)** What is the new equilibrium price? $ _____

(ii) What is the new equilibrium quantity?_____

d Explain what price you would suggest for movie tickets during the week to encourage more people to go to the movies.

_____

_____

_____

_____

      ISBN: 9780170415972

7 Use the information below to answer the questions that follow.

Market demand schedule for live crayfish	
Price $ per kg	Quantity demanded (kg)
20	5 000
40	4 000
60	3 000
80	1 000

North Island supply schedule for live crayfish	
Price $ per kg	Quantity supplied (kg)
20	1 000
40	2 000
60	2 500
80	2 750

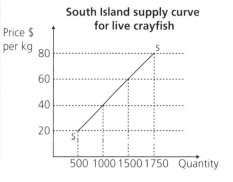

South Island supply curve for live crayfish

a On the grid below, draw the market demand and market supply curves for live crayfish in New Zealand.

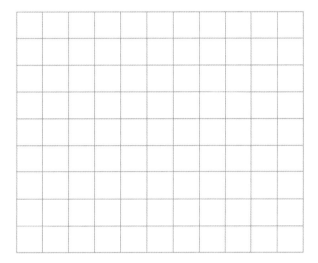

b Identify the equilibrium price and quantity on the graph as Pe and Qe respectively.

c **(i)** There has been an increase in the cost of diesel. Use the sketch graph below to show the effect of this increase on the market for live crayfish.

Market for live crayfish

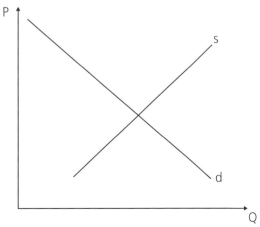

(ii) Explain how equilibrium is restored after the change.

_____

_____

_____

8 In the diagram below, 'C' represents the original equilibrium price and quantity for the coal market.

a For each situation below indicate which letter would represent the new equilibrium. (Always start at 'C'.)

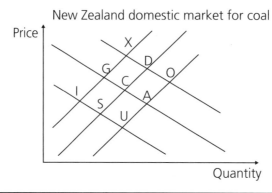

Situation	Letter answer
(i) An increase in demand	
(ii) An increase in supply	
(iii) A decrease in supply	
(iv) A decrease in demand	
(v) A new coal seam is discovered	
(vi) GST is raised to 15%	
(vii) Productivity in the coal industry is increased	
(viii) Cost of wages for coal miners increases	
(ix) The price of a complement decreases	
(x) Increased advertising for coal	
(xi) Direct tax is decreased	
(xii) New technology is used in the coal industry	
(xiii) A disaster at the coal mine and people's incomes decrease	
(xiv) The price of a substitute decreases and productivity in the coal industry decreases	

b (i) There has been a decrease in the cost of coal extraction. Use the sketch graph below to show the effect of this decrease on the market for coal.

(ii) Explain how equilibrium is restored after the change.

Market for coal

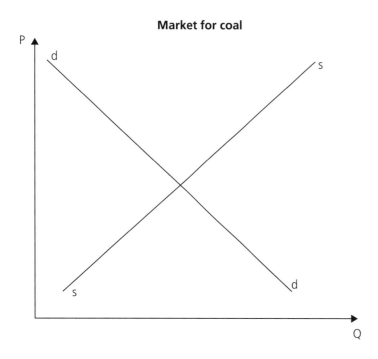

_____

_____

_____

_____

_____

_____

_____

_____

_____

_____

_____

 ISBN: 9780170415972

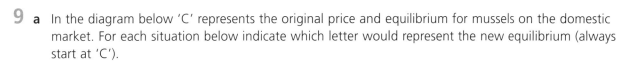

9 a In the diagram below 'C' represents the original price and equilibrium for mussels on the domestic market. For each situation below indicate which letter would represent the new equilibrium (always start at 'C').

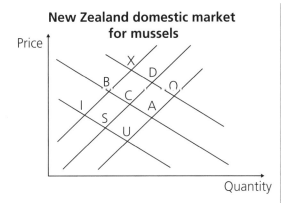

New Zealand domestic market for mussels

Situation	Letter answer
(i) An increase in GST to 17.5%	
(ii) An increase in productivity	
(III) A decrease in direct tax	
(iv) The price of a substitute decreases	
(v) Storms at sea keep boats tied up	
(vi) The price of a complement decreases and costs for the industry fall	
(vii) New technology is introduced into the industry and increased advertising for eating mussels	

b Write 'increase' or 'decrease' for the impact on equilibrium price and quantity for each situation indicated.

Situation	Impact on price	Impact on quantity
(i) A decrease in demand		
(ii) A decrease in supply		
(iii) Supply shifts to the left		
(iv) An increase in supply		
(v) Price of a substitute falls		
(vi) A subsidy is removed		
(vii) A tariff is imposed		
(viii) Price of related good falls		
(ix) Price of complement falls		

c On the graph below show the effect of a campaign that increases awareness of the benefits of eating mussels.

(i) Use dotted lines to indicate the new equilibrium price as P1 and new equilibrium quantity as Q1.

(ii) Explain how equilibrium is restored after the change.

Market for mussels

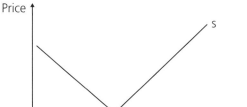

_____

_____

_____

_____

_____

_____

_____

_____

_____

Review (exam) questions

The health benefits of eating mussels has just been published in a medical journal, they contain a range of vitamins and have a low fat content.

1 **a** On the graph below, show the impact that is likely to result from the resource material above. Use dotted lines to show the new price and quantity. Fully label the changes.

Market for mussels monthly

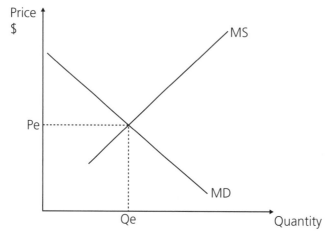

b Discuss how this information affects market demand. In your answer you should explain how market demand is determined and explain the effects this report will have on market demand.

_____

_____

_____

_____

_____

_____

_____

_____

_____

_____

_____

_____

_____

_____

_____

_____

_____

_____

_____

_____

       ISBN: 9780170415972

c Discuss the effect this change will have on the market for mussels monthly.
In your answer you should:

- explain the effect on mussel consumers
- explain the effect on mussel producers
- explain the effect on society.

_____

_____

_____

_____

_____

_____

_____

_____

_____

_____

_____

_____

_____

_____

_____

_____

_____

_____

_____

_____

_____

_____

_____

_____

_____

_____

_____

_____

_____

_____

_____

_____

_____

_____

More and more firms in the takeaway
industry are setting up to sell pizza.

2 a On the graph below, show the impact that is likely to result from the resource material above. Use dotted lines to show the new price and quantity. Fully label the changes.

Pizza market monthly

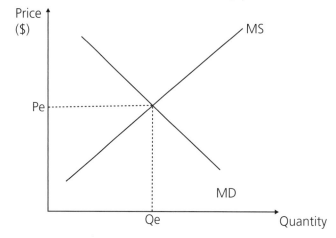

b Discuss how this information affects market supply. In your answer you should explain how market supply is determined and explain the effects the change indicated in the resource material will have on market supply.

_____

_____

_____

_____

_____

_____

_____

_____

_____

_____

_____

_____

_____

_____

_____

_____

_____

_____

_____

_____

_____

_____

PHOTOCOPYING OF THIS PAGE IS RESTRICTED UNDER LAW.   ISBN: 9780170415972

c Discuss the effect this change will have on the market for pizza monthly.
In your answer you should:

- explain the effect on pizza consumers
- refer to the graph.

_____

_____

_____

_____

_____

_____

_____

_____

_____

_____

_____

_____

_____

_____

_____

_____

_____

_____

_____

_____

_____

_____

_____

_____

_____

_____

_____

_____

_____

_____

_____

_____

_____

_____

_____

_____

_____

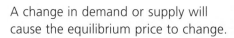

A change in demand or supply will
cause the equilibrium price to change.

3 a Complete the graph below to show ONE of the two ways that price may decrease, by labelling all curves. Show a price decrease of 20% for a cup of coffee. Use dotted lines to show the new equilibrium price (P1) and quantity (Q1)

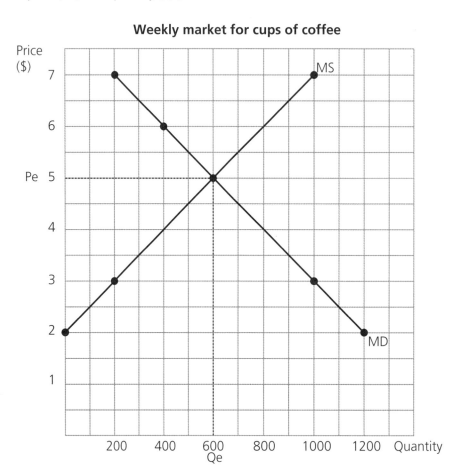

Weekly market for cups of coffee

_____

_____

_____

_____

_____

_____

_____

_____

_____

_____

_____

_____

_____

_____

_____

b Referring to the change you made on the graph above, fully explain how a new equilibrium is restored at P1 and Q1. In your answer you should:

- explain a possible cause for the change in demand OR supply shown in the graph
- how a new equilibrium can be reached
- data from the graph.

_____

_____

_____

_____

_____

_____

_____

_____

_____

_____

_____

_____

_____

_____

_____

_____

_____

_____

_____

_____

_____

_____

_____

_____

_____

_____

_____

_____

_____

_____

_____

_____

_____

_____

_____

11 SALES TAX AND THE MARKET

Sales tax and the market

An **indirect tax** (such as sales tax or VAT) is a tax collected by firms (a third party) and then passed on to the government. An indirect tax will decrease supply causing the equilibrium price to rise and equilibrium quantity to decrease. The advantages of a sales tax is that it decreases equilibrium quantity and the government raises revenue.

Illustrating a sales tax

To **illustrate the effects of a per unit (dollar) sales** tax requires shifting the original supply curve upward to the left by the per unit tax amount. For example, if the per unit tax is $7.50 and $7.50 equates to 3 spaces on the graph, you must shift the entire supply curve vertically upwards by this distance. It is important to note that the increase in the price will not be as much as the amount of the tax because the curves are sloping. Therefore, the producer is able to pass some of the tax on to the consumer.

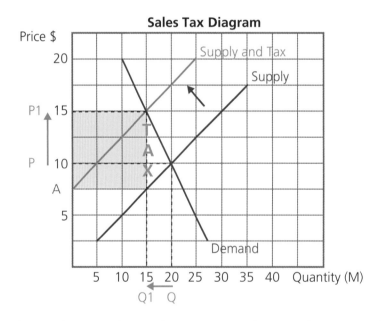

The tax per unit is the gap between the supply curves. Note the price does not rise by the full amount of the tax per unit. In this case the tax per unit is $7.50 but the price has gone up by $5.

P is the original price and **Q** is the original quantity

P1 is the new price and **Q1** is the new quantity

A is the price per item firms receive with an indirect tax

The impact of a sales tax worked example

	Before the tax	After the tax
Quantity sold	Q, 20m	Q1, 15m
Price consumers pay	P, $10	P1, $15
Consumer spending	P x Q, $200m	P1 x Q1, $225m
Price producers receive	P, $10	A, $7.50
Producer revenue	P x Q, $200m	A x Q1, $112.5m
Change in the value of sales	(P x Q) difference (P1 x Q1). An increase of $25m	
Change in producers' revenue	(P x Q) difference (A x Q1). A decrease of $87.5m	
How much is the tax per unit?	The size of the gap between the supply curves. $7.50	
Government revenue from the tax	Tax per unit x Q1. $7.50 x 15m = $112.5m	

The **incidence of a tax** refers to who actually pays the tax. In most cases, part of a tax is paid by the consumer and part is paid by the firm. **Consumers** pay to the extent of the price rise from the original price paid (P) to the new price paid (P1). Any amount of the tax not covered by the price increase has to be absorbed by the firm (from P to A on the diagram opposite).

The change in the value of consumer spending that results from the tax equals the difference between the original price a consumer pays (P) multiplied by the original quantity purchased (Q) and the new price paid (P1) multiplied by the new quantity purchased (Q1). Since a tax results in a price increase there will be a decrease in quantity demanded because fewer consumers are willing and able to purchase with their limited incomes.

The value of consumer spending may remain unchanged, decrease or increase because the new value of consumer spending depends on the relative changes in both the new price paid and the new quantity purchased. Consumers may look to buy a substitute good or service that is relatively cheaper.

Producers will find that the tax adds to their costs so they will decrease supply, meaning that there will be a decrease in quantity supplied at each and every price. The firm will collect the tax revenue and pass this onto the government. Therefore, the price per item firms receive with a tax will be lower than the price consumers pay for them.

To identify how much producers earn per item for the product at the new equilibrium you track down from the new equilibrium position until you hit the original supply curve, this gives the price per item firms receive with a tax (shown on the diagram as the letter A).

The change in the firm's income or revenue will be the difference between the firm's original income, which was the original price (P) received multiplied by the original quantity (Q) and the new value of the firm's income, which equals the price per item the firm now receives (A) multiplied by the new quantity sold (Q1).The producer's total income with the sales tax will fall because the price per item that the firm receives will be lower and the quantity sold will fall.

The revenue that the **government** collects from the tax equals the tax per unit multiplied by the new quantity (tax per unit x Q1). The tax revenue that the government collects is most likely to be used in a variety of different ways.

Student notes: Sales tax and the market

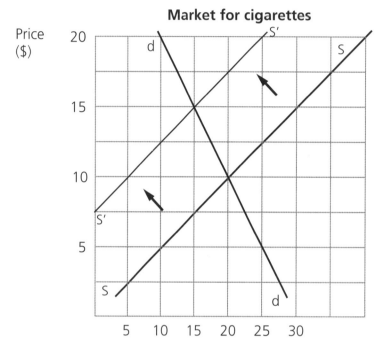

Market for cigarettes

Price ($)

20 — d — S'

S

15

10 — S'

5

S

d

5 10 15 20 25 30

Quantity (million)

1 Study the graph and answer the questions that follow.

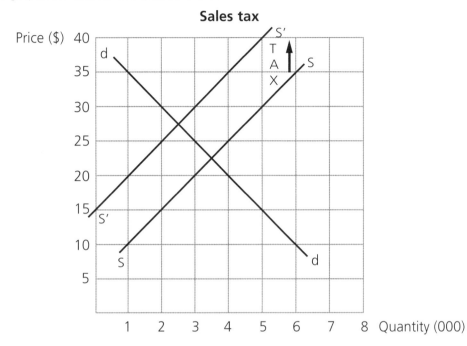

Sales tax

a On the above diagram label the original price P and original quantity Q. Label P' and Q' as the new equilibrium price and new equilibrium quantity respectively. Label the price firms receive with the sales tax as A.

b What is the value of the tax shown? _____

c Complete the table.

Question	Formula or letter	Value from graph
(i)	P	
(ii)	P'	
(iii)	A	
(iv)	P × Q	
(v)	P' × Q'	
(vi)	(P × Q) vs (P' × Q')	
(vii)	A × Q'	
(viii)	(A × Q') vs (P × Q)	
(ix)	Per unit tax × Q'	
(x)	Q	
(xi)	Q'	
(xii)	Q vs Q'	

2 Study the graph below and answer the questions that follow.

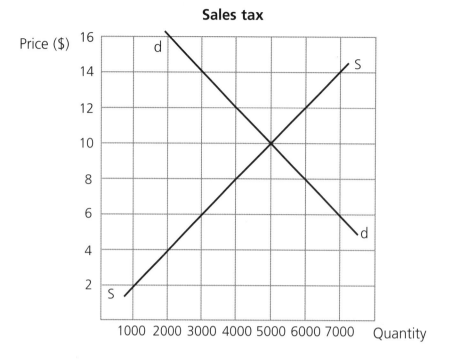

Sales tax

Price ($)

a Show on the above diagram a sales tax of $4 per item. Label the curve fully, showing the new price as P1 and the new quantity as Q1. Label the new price firms receive as Pp.

b Calculate the change in consumer spending following the imposition of the sales tax. Show your working.

_____

c What is the total income (revenue) producers would receive for producing the new equilibrium quantity?

_____

d What is the new equilibrium price?

_____

e At the new equilibrium how much do firms earn per item?

_____

f Calculate the change in firms' revenue following the imposition of the sales tax. Show your working.

_____

g Calculate the tax revenue collected by government. Show your working.

_____

3 Study the diagram and answer the questions that follow.

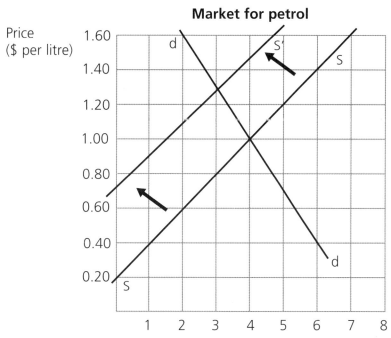

Market for petrol

Price ($ per litre)

a How much is the sales tax shown on the diagram? _____

b What is the new equilibrium price? _____

c At the new equilibrium what quantity is sold? _____

d At the new equilibrium how much do firms earn per item? _____

e Calculate the change in firms' income following the imposition of the sales tax. Show working.

_____

f Calculate the change in value of sales following the imposition of the sales tax. Show working.

_____

g Calculate the tax revenue collected by government. Show working.

_____

h Refer to the graph to explain the consequences of this tax on producers and consumers in New Zealand.

Producers: _____

_____

_____

_____

Consumers: _____

_____

_____

_____

_____

4 Study the diagram and answer the questions that follow.

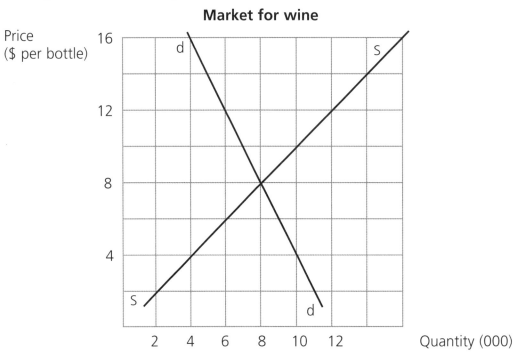

Market for wine

a Assume the government places a $6 sales tax on each bottle of wine. Draw and label the new curve in the graph.

b Referring to the graph, identify and calculate:

	Before the tax	After the tax
Quantity sold		
Price consumers pay		
Consumer spending		
Price producers receive		
Producer revenue		
Change in the value of sales		
Change in producers' revenue		
Government revenue from the tax		

5 Study the graph of the market for cartons of cigarettes and answer the questions that follow.

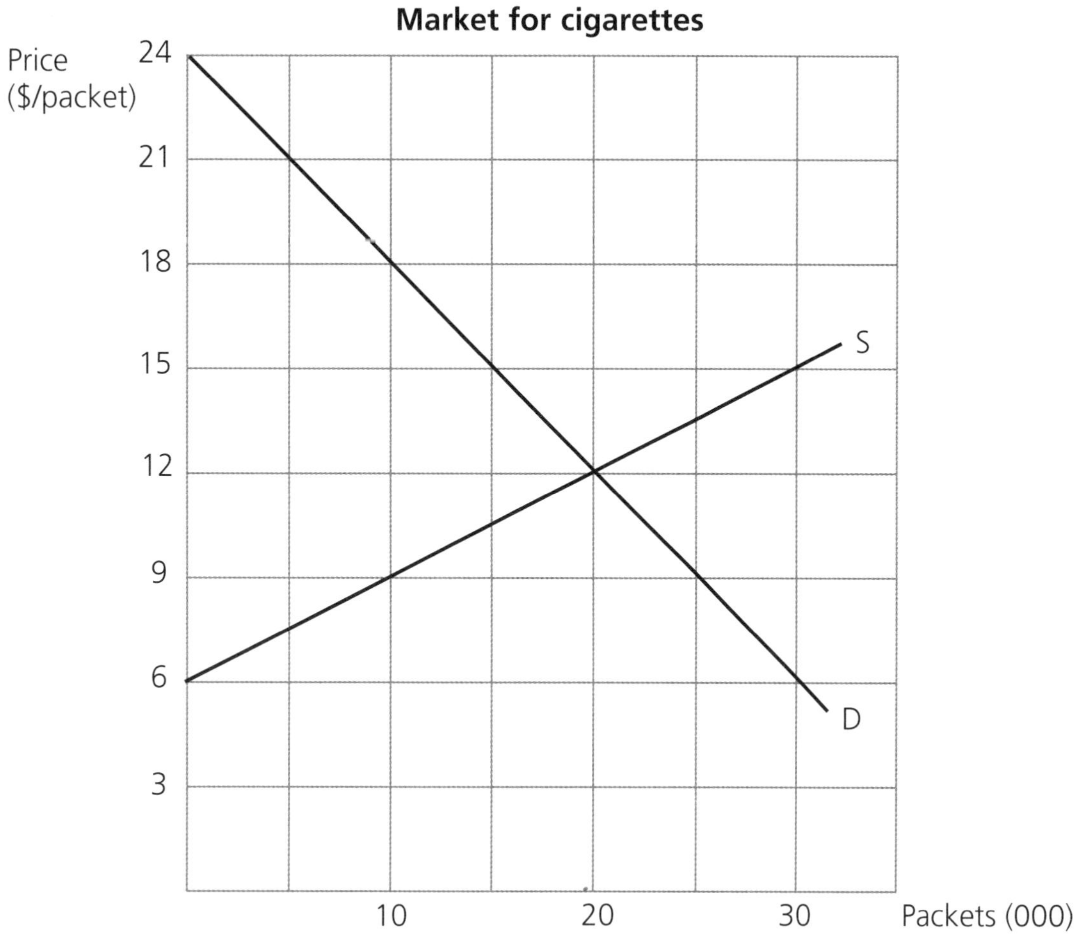

Market for cigarettes

a   Show the effect of a $4.50 per unit tax on the above diagram.

b   **(i)**   How much revenue does the tax raise for the government? (Show your calculation.)

_____

   (ii)   Shade in the area of tax revenue.

c   How much per packet do consumers now pay?   _____

d   What is the change in the value of sales?

_____

_____

e   Refer to the graph to explain the consequences of this tax on consumers and producers.

Consumers: _____

_____

Producers: _____

_____

_____

_____

Review (exam) questions

1 Study the graph and answer the questions that follow.

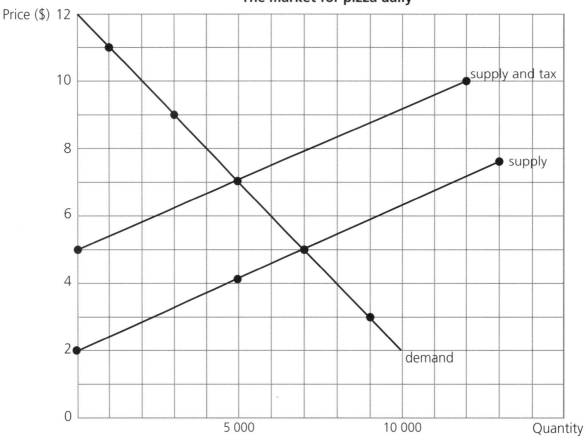

The market for pizza daily

a Referring to the graph, identify:

* the number of pizza consumers buy before and after tax

  before: _____ after: _____

* the price per pizza that consumers pay before and after tax

  before: _____ after: _____

* the price per pizza that producers receive before and after tax

  before: _____ after: _____

* the total tax revenue the government will earn from this tax (show your working).

  _____

b Explain fully how a tax on pizza might affect different sectors of the economy.
In your answer you should:

- explain the change in price to the consumer
- explain the change in price to the producer
- explain the immediate effect on the government
- explain any benefits to society
- refer to the graph above.

_____

_____

_____

_____

_____

_____

_____

_____

_____

_____

_____

_____

_____

_____

_____

_____

_____

_____

_____

_____

_____

_____

_____

_____

_____

_____

_____

_____

_____

_____

Concerns are being raised about the increased use of party pills. Government is set to review tax on party pills.

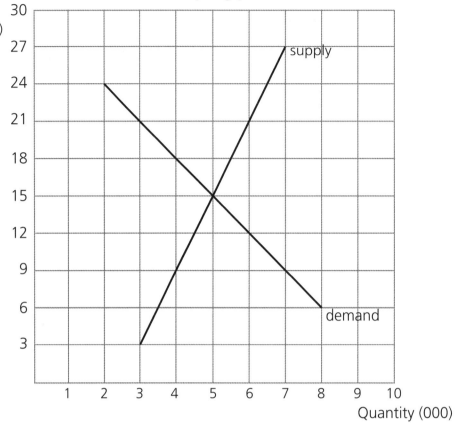

Market for party pills each week

2 **a** **(i)** On the graph above, show the original equilibrium price and quantity (label as Pe and Qe).

   (ii) Show the effect of a $9 per unit sales tax on party pills.

   (iii) Show the new equilibrium price and quantity (label as P1 and Q1).

b Refer to the graph and identify:

  • the number of party pills consumers buy before and after the sales tax

    before: _____ after: _____

  • the price per packet of party pills consumers pay before and after the sales tax

    before: _____ after: _____

  • the price per packet of party pills firms receive before and after the sales tax

    before: _____ after: _____

c Explain fully how a tax on party pills might affect different sectors of the economy.
In your answer you should:

- explain the change in price to the consumer
- explain the change in price to the producer
- explain the immediate effect on the government
- explain any benefits to society
- refer to the graph above.

_____

_____

_____

_____

_____

_____

_____

_____

_____

_____

_____

_____

_____

_____

_____

_____

_____

_____

_____

_____

_____

_____

_____

_____

_____

_____

_____

_____

_____

Alcohol sales continue to soar and drink-related crimes are on the increase.

Market for 1-litre bottles of vodka monthly

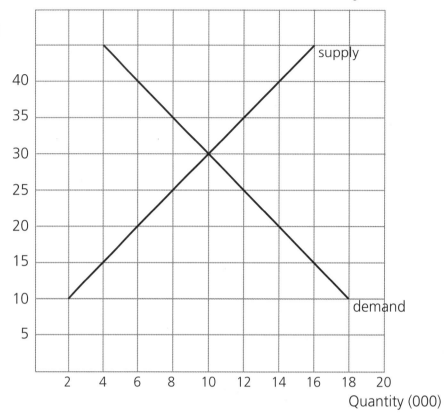

Price (per 1-litre bottle)

Quantity (000)

3 **a** **(i)** On the graph above, show the original equilibrium price and quantity (label as Pe and Qe)..

(ii) Show the effect of a $10 per unit sales tax on a 1-litre bottle of vodka.

(iii) Show the new equilibrium price and quantity (label as P1 and Q1).

b Refer to the graph and identify:

- the number of 1-litre bottles of vodka consumers buy before and after the sales tax

  before: _____

  after: _____

- the price per litre bottle of vodka consumers pay before and after the sales tax

  before: _____

  after: _____

- the price per litre bottle of vodka firms receive before and after the sales tax

  before: _____

  after: _____

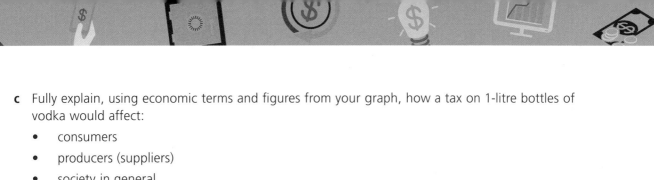

c Fully explain, using economic terms and figures from your graph, how a tax on 1-litre bottles of vodka would affect:

-   consumers
-   producers (suppliers)
-   society in general.

_____

_____

_____

_____

_____

_____

_____

_____

_____

_____

_____

_____

_____

_____

_____

_____

_____

_____

_____

_____

_____

_____

_____

_____

_____

_____

_____

_____

_____

_____

_____

12 SUBSIDY AND THE MARKET

Subsidy and the market

A **subsidy** is a payment by government to firms to keep their costs down, and as a result firms will increase supply. As supply increases the equilibrium price will decrease and the equilibrium quantity will increase.

Illustrating a subsidy

To **illustrate the effects of a per unit (dollar) subsidy** requires shifting the original supply curve downward to the right by the per unit subsidy amount. For example, if the per unit subsidy is $20 and $20 equates to 4 spaces on the graph, you must shift the entire supply curve vertically downwards this distance. It is important to note that the decrease in the price will not be as much as the amount of the subsidy because the curves are sloping. In most cases part of the subsidy will benefit the consumer and part will benefit the firm.

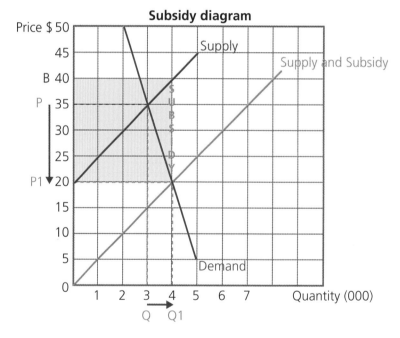

The subsidy per unit is the gap between the supply curves. Note the price does not fall by the full amount of the subsidy per unit. In this case the subsidy per unit is $20 but the price has gone down by $15.

P is the original price and **Q** is the original quantity

P1 is the new price and **Q1** is the new quantity

B is the price per item firms receive with a subsidy

The impact of a subsidy worked example

	Before the subsidy	After the subsidy
Quantity sold	Q, 3 000	Q1, 4 000
Price consumers pay	P, $35	P1, $20
Consumer spending	P x Q, $105 000	P1 x Q1, $80 000
Price producers receive	P, $35	B, $40
Producer revenue	P x Q, $105 000	B x Q1, $160 000
Change in the value of sales	(P x Q) difference (P1 x Q1). A decrease of $25 000	
Change in producers' revenue	(P x Q) difference (B x Q1). An increase of $55 000	
How much is the subsidy per unit?	The size of the gap between the supply curves. $20	
Costs to the government of the subsidy	Subsidy per unit x Q1. $20 x 4 000 = $80 000	

The **incidence of a subsidy** is a reference to who actually benefits from the government paying a subsidy. **Consumers** benefit to the extent of the price decreases from the original price paid (P) to the new price they pay (P1). Any amount of the subsidy not covered by the price decrease to consumers goes to the firm (from P to B on the diagram opposite).

The change in the value of consumer spending that results from the subsidy equals the difference between the original price a consumer pays (P) multiplied by the original quantity purchased (Q) and the new price paid (P1) multiplied by the new quantity purchased (Q1). Since a subsidy results in a price decrease there will be an increase in quantity demanded because more consumers are more willing and able to purchase the good or service with their limited incomes.

The value of consumer spending may remain unchanged, decrease or increase because the new value of consumer spending depends on the relative changes in both the new price paid and the new quantity purchased. Consumers may look to buy a complement to use in conjunction with the subsidied good or service. Consumers may also look to buy less of a substitute good or service that is relatively more expensive. Individuals who are involved in an industry that receives a subsidy may get more overtime and their disposable incomes will increase.

Producers will find that the subsidy reduces their costs so they will increase supply, meaning that there will be an increase in quantity supplied at each and every price. The price per item that firms receive with a subsidy will be higher than the price that consumers pay them. To identify how much producers earn per item for the product you track up from the new equilibrium position until you hit the original supply curve, this gives the price per item firms receive with a subsidy (shown on the diagram as the letter B).

The change in the firm's income or revenue will be the difference between the firm's original income, which was the original price (P) received, multiplied by the original quantity (Q) and the new value of the firm's income, which equals the price per item the firm now receives (B) multiplied by the new quantity sold (Q1). The producer's total income with the subsidy will increase because the price per item that the firm receives will be higher and the quantity sold will increase. Given this a firm may be more confident about the future and hire additional workers, pay overtime or invest in new machinery. New firms may enter the industry or existing firms switch additional resources into producing the subsidied good or service (from a related good).

The cost to the **government** of the subsidy equals the subsidy per unit multiplied by the new quantity (subsidy per unit x Q1). The money that the government spends on providing the subsidy means that other areas of spending are foregone.

The **advantage of a subsidy** over price controls is that equilibrium quantity will increase and there will be no shortage as is the case with a maximum price. A subsidy is an artificial means of reducing the comparative costs between domestic and foreign producers. A subsidy is a payment made by the government to a firm, which in effect lowers production costs. It enables a domestic producer to supply a greater quantity than would be the case otherwise. As the price falls, foreign producers find it more difficult to compete against the lower-priced domestic product.

The **disadvantage of a subsidy** is that it may be very expensive for the government, and legislation is a cheaper option (not costless because there are enforcement costs). With a subsidy, the government has to spend money which has to be paid out of taxes. A subsidy will cost the government money and has an opportunity cost that this money could be spent on something else, it may support inefficient producers. A subsidy may cause domestic producers to become inefficient and may remove the incentive to innovate or become more efficient.

Student notes: Subsidy and the market

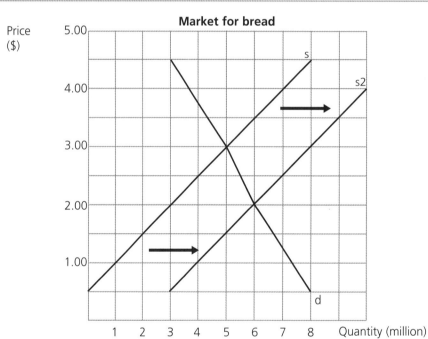

Market for bread

1 Study the graph and answer the questions that follow.

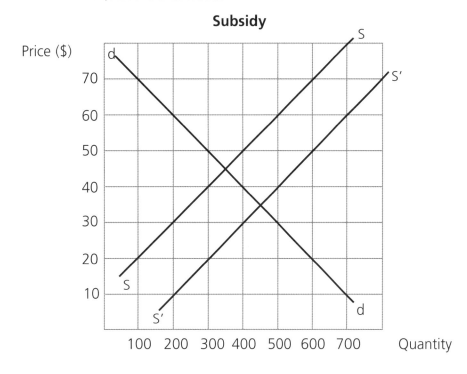

Subsidy

Price ($)

a On the above diagram label the original price P and new price P'. Label the original quantity Q and new quantity Q'. Label the price firms receive with a subsidy as B.

b What is the value of the subsidy shown? _____

c Complete the table below.

Question	Formula or letter	Value from graph
(i)	P	
(ii)	P'	
(iii)	P × Q	
(iv)	P' × Q'	
(v)	(P × Q) vs (P' × Q')	
(vi)	P × Q	
(vii)	B × Q'	
(viii)	(P × Q) vs (B × Q')	
(ix)	B	
(x)	subsidy per unit × Q'	
(xi)	Q	
(xii) Quantity sold after		

2 Study the diagram below and answer the questions that follow.

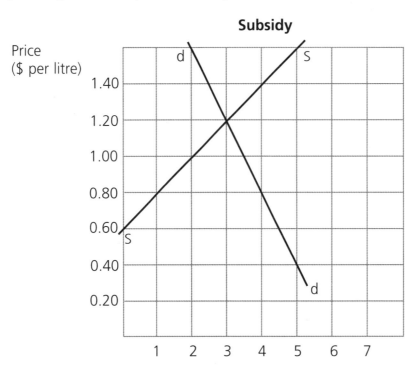

Subsidy

Price ($ per litre)

Quantity (million litres)

a Draw and label a new supply curve to show a subsidy of $0.60 per litre on the above diagram.

b Work out the new equilibrium price. _____

c Work out the new equilibrium quantity. _____

d Work out the change in the value of sales.

_____

_____

e At the new equilibrium how much do firms earn per item? _____

f Calculate the change in firms' income following the subsidy. Show working.

_____

_____

g Calculate the cost to the government of the subsidy. _____

h What is a subsidy?

_____

_____

_____

3 Study the diagram and answer the questions that follow.

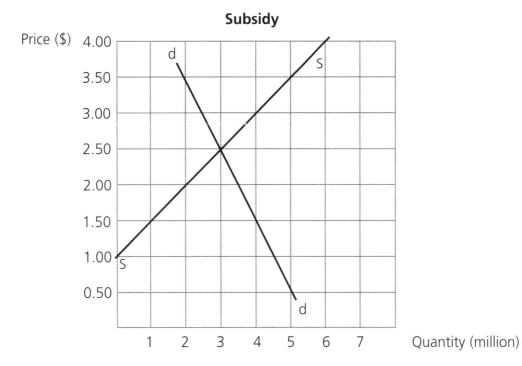

Subsidy

a Assume the government gives $1.50 subsidy on each item. Draw and label the new curve in the graph.

b Referring to the graph, identify and calculate:

	Before the subsidy	**After the subsidy**
Quantity sold		
Price consumers pay		
Consumer spending		
Price producers receive		
Producer revenue		
Change in the value of sales		
Change in producers' revenue		
Cost to the government of the subsidy		

c State the advantage of a subsidy over a price control.

_____

_____

_____

_____

_____

4 A study has determined that crayfish numbers are at record levels. As a result of this the government has given a subsidy to catch crayfish.

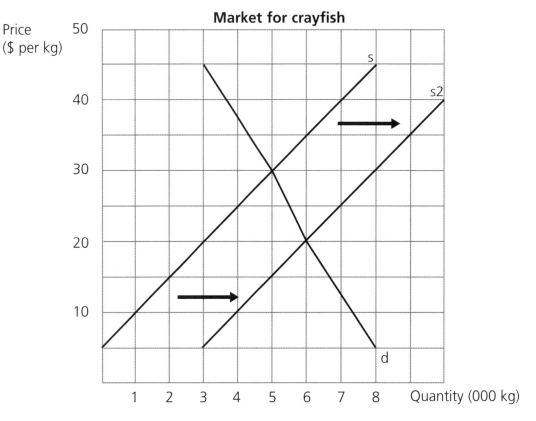

Market for crayfish

a **(i)** What is the amount of the subsidy per unit? _____

   (ii) Calculate the cost to the government of this subsidy.

   _____

   (iii) What price does the producer now receive?

   _____

   (iv) What is total consumer spending after the subsidy?

   _____

b Refer to the graph to explain the consequences of this subsidy on producers and consumers in New Zealand.

   Producers: _____

   _____

   _____

   _____

   Consumers: _____

   _____

   _____

   _____

5 Study the graph and answer the questions that follow.

a Draw a per unit subsidy of $15 on the graph below.

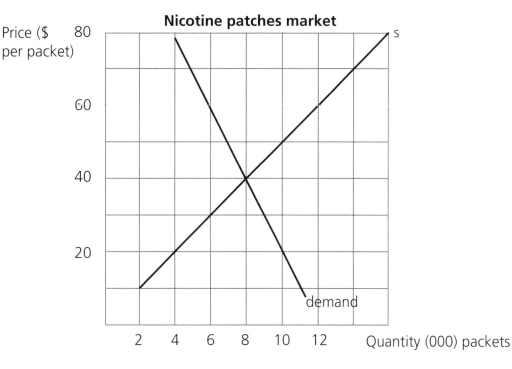

Nicotine patches market

Price ($ per packet)

Quantity (000) packets

b Referring to the graph, identify:

- the price that consumers pay before and after the subsidy

before: _____ after: _____

- the price that producers receive before and after the subsidy

before: _____ after: _____

- the quantity that consumers buy before and after the subsidy.

before: _____ after: _____

- Calculate how much this subsidy costs the Government in total (show your working).

_____

c Explain the flow-on effects for society.

_____

_____

_____

_____

_____

_____

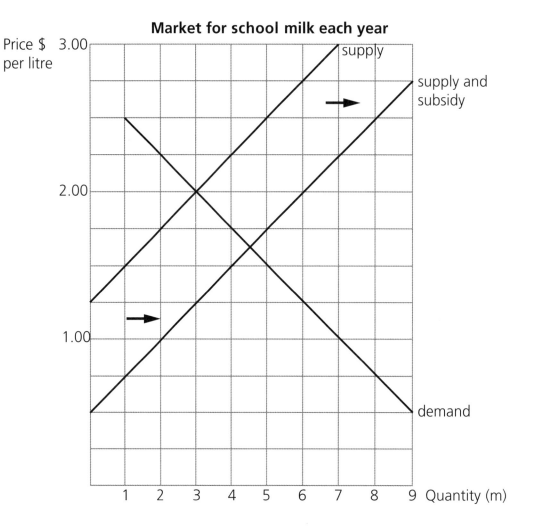

Market for school milk each year

6 **a** **(i)** Label the original price and quantity as Pe and Qe respectively.

(ii) Label the new price consumers pay as Pc.

(iii) Label the price per item firms now receive as Pp.

(iv) Label the new equilibrium quantity as Q1.

(v) Shade and label the total cost to the government of the subsidy.

b How much is the subsidy per unit?

_____

c Calculate the cost to the government of the subsidy.

_____

d How would this subsidy affect producers?

_____

_____

_____

_____

_____

_____

To help reduce the congestion on the roads, local councils have decided to subsidise bus fares.

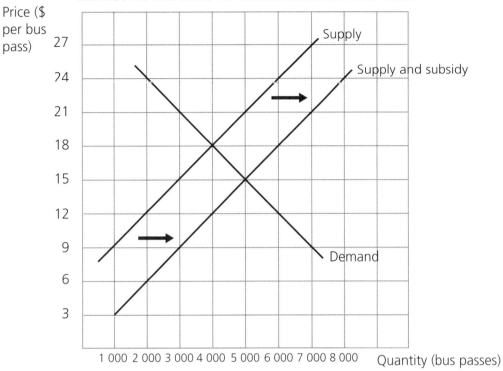

Market for bus fares for school students each week

7 Fully explain, using economic terms and figures from the graph, how a subsidy on bus fares would affect:
- consumers
- producers (suppliers)
- society in general.

_____

_____

_____

_____

_____

_____

_____

_____

_____

_____

_____

_____

_____

_____

_____

Review (exam) questions

Many drink-drivers will not use a
taxi because the cost is too high.

1 a Show the effects of a per-unit subsidy of $15 on taxi rides.

Taxi market daily

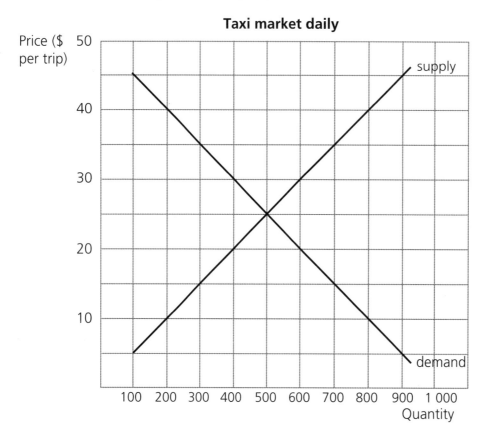

b Referring to the graph, identify:

• the number of trips consumers take before and after the subsidy

before: _____   after: _____

• the price per trip consumers pay before and after the subsidy

before: _____   after: _____

• the price per trip producers receive before and after the subsidy

before: _____   after: _____

• the total cost of the subsidy to the government.

_____

c Fully explain, using economic terms and figures from your graph, how a subsidy on taxi rides would affect:
- consumers
- producers (suppliers)
- society in general.

_____

_____

_____

_____

_____

_____

_____

_____

_____

_____

_____

_____

_____

_____

_____

_____

_____

_____

_____

_____

_____

_____

_____

_____

_____

_____

_____

_____

_____

_____

Drownings on the increase, many
boaties still not wearing lifejackets.

Market for lifejackets each month

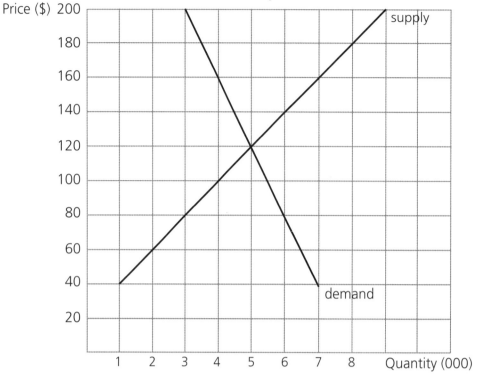

2 **a** **(i)** On the graph above, show the original equilibrium price and quantity (label as Pe and Qe).

(ii) Show the effect of a $60 per unit subsidy on lifejackets.

(iii) Show the new equilibrium price and quantity (label as P1 and Q1).

b Refer to the graph and identify:

* the number of lifejackets consumers buy before and after the subsidy

  before: _____ after: _____

* the price per lifejacket consumers pay before and after the subsidy

  before: _____ after: _____

* the price per lifejacket firms receive before and after the subsidy

  before: _____ after: _____

c Fully explain how a subsidy on lifejackets might affect different sectors of the economy.
In your answer you should:
- explain the change in price to the consumer
- explain the change in price to the producer
- explain the immediate effect on the government
- explain any benefits to society
- refer to the graph above.

The cancer society is still concerned that many individuals have not got the 'cover up' message …

Market for sunhats each week

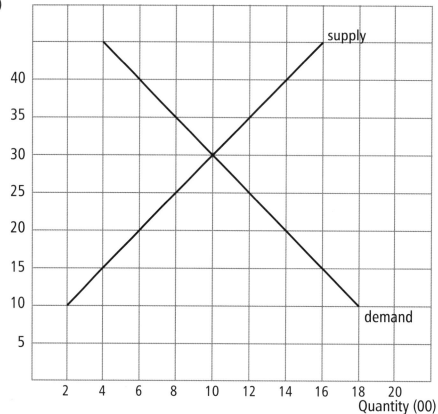

3 a (i) On the graph above, show the original equilibrium price and quantity (label as Pe and Qe).

(ii) Show the effect of a $10 per unit subsidy on sunhats.

(iii) Show the new equilibrium price and quantity (label as P1 and Q1).

b Refer to the graph and identify:

- the number of sunhats consumers buy before and after the subsidy

before: _____ after: _____

- the price per sunhats consumers pay before and after the subsidy

before: _____ after: _____

- the price per sunhat firms receive before and after the subsidy

before: _____ after: _____

ISBN: 9780170415972

c Explain fully how a subsidy on sunhats might affect different sectors of the economy.
In your answer you should:
- explain the change in price to the consumer
- explain the change in price to the producer
- explain the immediate effect on the government
- explain any benefits to society
- refer to the graph above.

_____

_____

_____

_____

_____

_____

_____

_____

_____

_____

_____

_____

_____

_____

_____

_____

_____

_____

_____

_____

_____

_____

_____

_____

_____

_____

_____

_____

_____

Maximum price control (ceiling price)

A **price control** (maximum or minimum price) is imposed by government so that price cannot automatically move back to the equilibrium as it would in the free market because laws or regulations prohibit this.

A **maximum price** (or **ceiling price**) is a price control set by government prohibiting the charging of a price higher than a certain level. A maximum price is set in the interests of consumers to protect them from paying unreasonably high prices for essential goods and services, for example housing, petrol or certain food items such as bread and milk.

Illustrating a maximum price

To illustrate the effects of a maximum price, draw a line at the price at which the maximum price is set and label this appropriately. Draw a dotted line to show the quantity demanded (Qd) and quantity supplied (Qs) at this price, than label the resulting shortage created. Show the decrease in price from the original price (Pe) to the maximum price (Pmax)

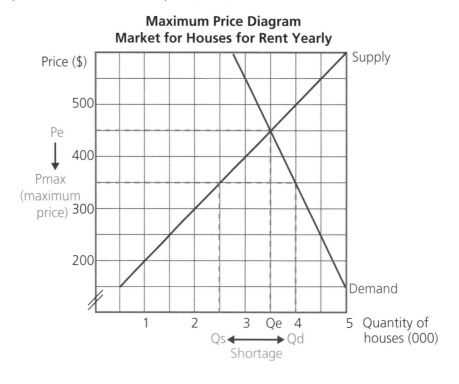

Pe is the original price and **Qe** is the original quantity

Qd is the new quantity demanded by consumers after the maximum price.

Qs is the new quantity supplied by producers after the maximum price.

The impact of a maximum price worked example

	Before the maximum price	After the maximum price
Quantity sold	Qe, 3 500	Qs, 2 500
Price consumers pay	Pe, $450	Pmax, $350
Consumer spending	Pe x Qe, $1 575 000	Pmax x Qs, $875 000
Price producers receive	Pe, $450	Pmax, $350
Producer revenue	Pe x Qe, $1 575 000	Pmax x Qs, $875 000
Size of the shortage	The size of the gap between Qs and Qd. 1 500 houses	
Change in the value of sales	(Pe x Qe) difference (Qs x Pmax). A decrease of $700 000	
Change in producers' revenue	(Pe x Qe) difference (Qs x Pmax). A decrease of $700 000	

If the government sets a maximum price control of $350 for the market of houses to rent this restricts the rent that landlords are legally allowed to charge tenants. The diagram shows that imposing a maximum price at $350 for a house to rent will cause the price to fall from $450 to $350. As the price decreases the quantity demanded of houses by consumers (potential tenants) increases from 3 500 (Qe) to 4 000 (Qd), while the quantity supplied of houses made available to rent by landlords decreases from 3 500 (Qe) to 2 500 (Qs). This causes a shortage of 1 500 houses to rent and could give rise to a black market where some people are willing to pay a higher price than the legally set price by government of $350 to rent a house.

The change in total value of sales after the maximum price is imposed is the difference between the original price multiplied by the original quantity (Pe multiplied by Qe) and the maximum price set multiplied by the quantity made available by suppliers (Maximum Price multiplied by Qs). In this instance, it is the difference between ($450 multiplied by 3 500) and ($350 multiplied by 2 500) which is the difference between $1 575 000 and $875 000, a $700 000 decrease.

To assist individuals and families moving into affordable housing the government could increase the supply of houses to rent by offering landlords a subsidy. A subsidy is a payment by government to suppliers (businesses) to keep costs down, as a result they will increase supply and the price will decrease. The advantage of a subsidy over a maximum price control is that there will be no shortage and the market will clear. The disadvantage of a subsidy is that it may be very expensive for the government, and the money spent on the subsidised good or services means this money cannot be spent elsewhere.

A maximum price set above the equilibrium price has no effect because a price above the equilibrium price creates a surplus (excess supply) where market forces automatically cause the price to decrease back to the equilibrium. Therefore, to be effective, a maximum price must be set below the equilibrium.

The **advantages of a maximum price** control is that it will lower the price of the good or service and make it more affordable for consumers, and there is no cost to the government. The problem of an effective maximum price set below the equilibrium is that it distorts the market because it does not allow the market to clear. A maximum price set below the equilibrium results in a shortage (excess demand), because at prices below the equilibrium the quantity demanded by consumers is greater than the quantity supplied by producers. This means that some consumers who had the good or service before the maximum price was imposed miss out because the quantity supplied decreases as the price falls. Solutions to overcome the shortage created by a maximum price could be first-come-first-served until supply runs out, or the government could issue ration cards giving an equal share to everyone.

A **black market** can arise with a maximum price. A black market is part of the underground or informal economy where activities that take place are illegal, unregulated and not taxed. In a black market, firms charge a price above the legally set government maximum price or well-off customers or consumers pay more than the government's legally set price or obtain the good or service that circumvents rationing measures put in place by the government.

Student notes: Price controls – Maximum price

   ISBN: 9780170415972

QUESTIONS & TASKS

1 Study the following graph and answer the questions that follow.

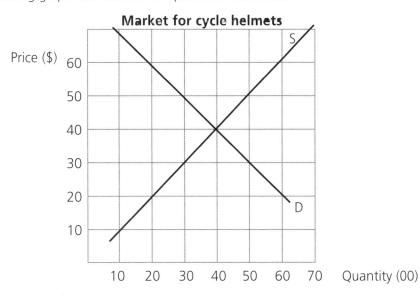

Market for cycle helmets

a Identify the equilibrium price and equilibrium quantity.

    (i) Equilibrium price: $_____   **(ii)** Equilibrium quantity: _____

b Name the price at which a surplus of 2 000 cycle helmets will occur.

    $ _____

c What is a price control?

    _____

    _____

    _____

    _____

    _____

d On the graph above, show a maximum price that is set 25% below the equilibrium price.

e Calculate the change in quantity supplied as a result of the maximum price.

    _____

f Calculate the revenue for producers at the equilibrium price, and at the maximum price. (Show your working.)

    (i) Revenue at equilibrium price: _____

    (ii) Revenue at maximum price: _____

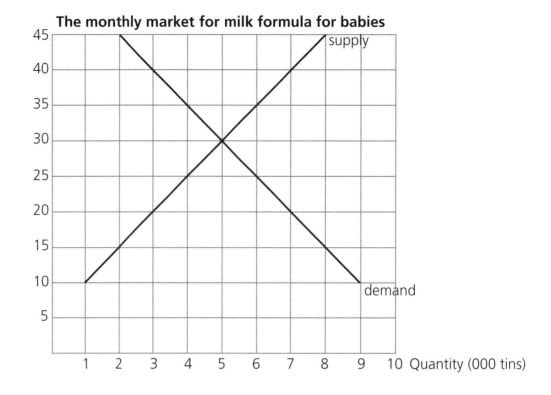

The monthly market for milk formula for babies

Price $ per tin (y-axis): 5, 10, 15, 20, 25, 30, 35, 40, 45

Quantity (000 tins) (x-axis): 1, 2, 3, 4, 5, 6, 7, 8, 9, 10

supply

demand

2 **a** On the monthly market for milk formula for babies graph above, show the effect of a maximum price control that reduces the price by 25%. You must label the maximum price (Pmax), the quantity demanded (Qd) and quantity supplied (Qs).

  b Referring to the graph in **a**, fully explain the consequences of a maximum price control on this market. Include the following in your explanation:
  - quantity demanded before and after the maximum price control
  - quantity supplied before and after the maximum price control
  - a problem the maximum price control might create
  - a possible solution for the above problem.

_____

_____

_____

_____

_____

_____

_____

_____

_____

_____

_____

_____

_____

_____

3 Study the graph 'Market for school shoes' and answer the questions that follow.

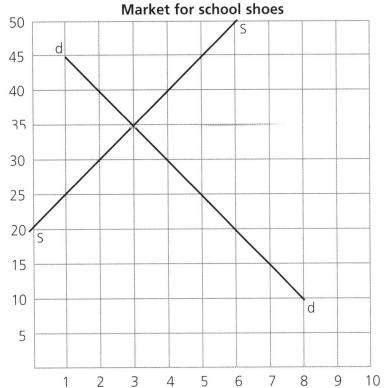

Market for school shoes

Price ($ per pair of shoes) — vertical axis

Quantity (000) — horizontal axis

a **(i)** How much would the subsidy have to be per pair of shoes for the price to fall to $25?

_____

(ii) On the diagram show the effect of a subsidy that results in a price of $25 per pair of shoes. Label the new equilibrium quantity Q'.

b **(i)** What price does the producer receive after the subsidy?

_____

(ii) What is total consumer spending after the subsidy? _____

(iii) Calculate the cost to the government of such a subsidy. _____

c State the advantage of subsidies over price controls.

_____

_____

d A maximum price could have achieved a market price of $25 but will have a different effect on quantity supplied than a subsidy. For a maximum price and the subsidy calculate the change in quantity supplied.

Maximum price control option _____

Subsidy option _____

4 Use the diagram below to answer the questions that follow.

Market for houses for rent

The government wants to reduce the cost of houses for rent. One option is to impose a price control of $175.

a What is the correct economic term for this option?

_____

b Show the effect on the graph of the government imposing a price control of $175.

c Alternatively, the government could achieve the same market price of $175 by offering a subsidy. How much would the subsidy on each house have to be?

_____

d Calculate the cost of the subsidy to the government.

_____

e Both price control and subsidy options achieve the same market price but have different effects on the quantity supplied. For each option calculate the change in quantity supplied.

(i) price control option _____ **(ii)** subsidy option _____

f State one advantage of subsidies over price controls.

_____

_____

 ISBN: 9780170415972

5 The government is considering ways to improve the health and well-being of the nation. It is considering a maximum price control (with the price set below equilibrium) or a subsidy for gym membership.

a Describe and explain the advantages and disadvantages of a subsidy.

Advantages: _____

_____

_____

_____

_____

Disadvantages: _____

_____

_____

_____

b Describe and explain the advantages and disadvantages of a maximum price control.

_____

_____

_____

_____

_____

_____

_____

_____

_____

_____

_____

c Explain whether it is better for the government to use a subsidy or a maximum price control.

_____

_____

_____

_____

_____

_____

_____

Review (exam) questions

The government is considering a ceiling price for milk.

1 **a** Show the effects of a maximum price of $2.20 per litre on the graph below (labelled as Pmax) on the market for milk each week.

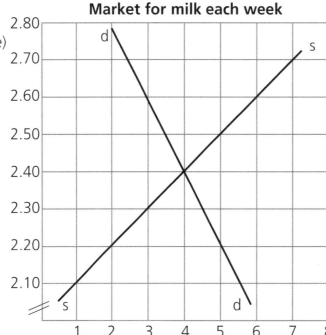

Market for milk each week

Price ($ per litre) — vertical axis: 2.80, 2.70, 2.60, 2.50, 2.40, 2.30, 2.20, 2.10

Quantity (million litres) — horizontal axis: 1, 2, 3, 4, 5, 6, 7, 8

b Referring to the graph, identify:

- the price that consumers pay before and after the maximum price

  before: _____ after: _____

- the price that producers receive before and after the maximum price

  before: _____ after: _____

- the quantity that consumers buy before and after the maximum price

  before: _____ after: _____

- the value of sales before and after the maximum price

  before: _____

  after: _____

c Fully explain the effects of introducing a maximum price on milk consumers.
In your answer you should:
- explain the change in price
- explain the change in quantity demanded
- explain the change in consumer spending on milk
- explain two flow-on effects on society in general
- refer to the data above.

_____

_____

_____

_____

_____

_____

_____

_____

_____

_____

_____

_____

_____

_____

_____

_____

_____

_____

_____

_____

_____

_____

_____

_____

_____

_____

_____

_____

_____

2 a Show the effects on the market for taxi rides per day of a maximum price for taxi rides of $20 per trip (label as Pmax).

You must:

- use dotted lines to show the equilibrium price (Pe) and quantity (Qe) before the maximum price
- use dotted lines to show the new quantity demanded (Qd) and quantity supplied (Qs) after the maximum price
- fully label the resulting surplus or shortage.

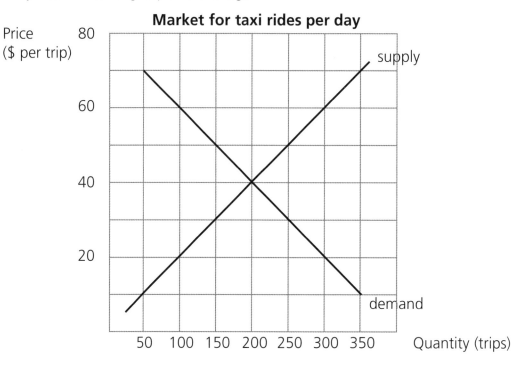

Market for taxi rides per day

b Referring to the graph, identify:

- the price that consumers pay before and after the maximum price

  before: _____ after: _____

- the price that producers receive before and after the maximum price

  before: _____ after: _____

- the quantity of trips that consumers buy before and after the maximum price

  before: _____ after: _____

- the firms' revenue before and after the maximum price

  before: _____

  after: _____

c Fully explain the effects of introducing a maximum price on taxi rides for consumers.
   In your answer you should:

   • explain the change in price
   • explain the change in quantity demanded
   • explain the change in consumer spending on taxi rides
   • explain two flow-on effects on society in general
   • refer to the data above.

_____

_____

_____

_____

_____

_____

_____

_____

_____

_____

_____

_____

_____

_____

_____

_____

_____

_____

_____

_____

_____

_____

_____

_____

_____

_____

_____

_____

_____

_____

_____

_____

_____

_____

Minimum price control (floor price)

A **price control** (maximum or minimum price) is imposed by government so that price cannot automatically move back to the equilibrium as it would in the free market because laws or regulations prohibit this.

A **minimum price (or floor price)** is a price control set by government where the market price is not allowed to fall below a certain minimum (floor) level. A minimum price is set by the government in the interests of producers to protect them from volatile prices in world markets and ensure that they are not receiving an unreasonably low price for what they produce. At one time in New Zealand, the government set a minimum (floor) price on wool and butter.

Illustrating a minimum price

To illustrate the effects of a minimum price, draw a line at the price at which the minimum price is set and label this appropriately. Draw a dotted line to show the quantity demanded (Qd) and quantity supplied (Qs) at this price, than label the resulting surplus created. Show the increase in price from the original price (Pe) to the minimum price (Pmin)

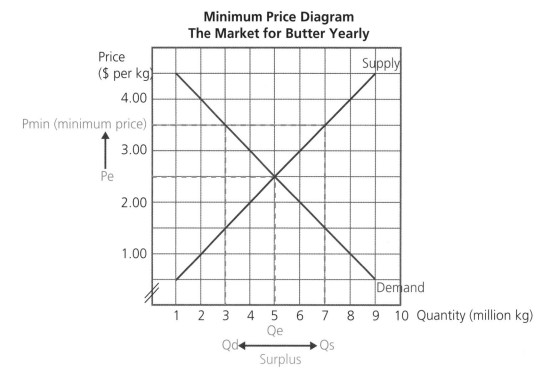

Minimum Price Diagram
The Market for Butter Yearly

Pe is the original price and **Qe** is the original quantity

Qd is the new quantity demanded by consumers after the minimum price.

Qs is the new quantity supplied by producers after the minimum price.

The impact of a minimum price worked example

	Before the minimum price	After the minimum price
Quantity sold	Qe, 5 million kg	Qd, 3 million kg
Price consumers pay	Pe, $2.50 per kg	Pmin, $3.50 per kg
Consumer spending	Pe x Qe, $12.5m	Pmin x Qd, $10.5m
Price producers receive	Pe, $2.50 per kg	Pmin, $3.50 per kg
Producer revenue	Pe x Qe, $12.5m	Pmin x Qs, $24.5m
Size of the surplus	The size of the gap between Qd and Qs. 4 million kg of butter	
Change in the value of sales	(Pe x Qe) difference (Pmin x Qd). A decrease of $2m	
Change in producers' revenue	(Pe x Qe) difference (Pmin x Qs). An increase of $12m	

If the government sets a minimum price control of $3.50 per kg on the market for butter, the diagram shows, the price of butter will increase from $2.50 per kg to $3.50 per kg. As the price increases the quantity of butter demanded by consumers decreases from 5 million kg (Qe) to 3 million kg (Qd), while the quantity of butter supplied by firms increases from 5 million kg (Qe) to 7 million kg (Qs). This causes a surplus of 4 million kg of butter that the government has to buy and store.

The change in total value of sales after the minimum price is imposed is the difference between the original price multiplied by the original quantity (Pe multiplied by Qe) and the minimum price set multiplied by the quantity purchased by consumers (Minimum Price multiplied by Qd). In this instance, it is the difference between ($2.50 multiplied by 5m) and ($3.50 multiplied by 3m) which is the difference between $12.5m and $10.5m, a $2m decrease.

The change in a firms revenue is the difference between the original price multiplied by the original quantity (Pe multiplied by Qe) and the minimum price set multiplied by the quantity produced by producers (Minimum Price multiplied by Qs). In this instance, it is the difference between ($2.50 multiplied by 5m) and ($3.50 multiplied by 7m) which is the difference between $12.5m and $24.5m, an increase of $12 million.

To be effective, a minimum price is set above the equilibrium price. This encourages producers to increase the quantity supplied because they are more able to cover their costs because they are earning higher revenue and it is more profitable to produce the good or service. The problem of an effective minimum price set above the equilibrium is that it distorts the market because it does not allow the market to clear. At the higher price the quantity demanded by consumers is less than the quantity supplied by producers resulting in excess supply (a surplus). The surplus (excess supply) is created because price is not allowed to fall below the controlled price to the equilibrium. The government then has to decide what to do with the surplus stock. In the past this surplus stock was stockpiled and sold at a later date.

A minimum price set below the equilibrium price has no effect because a price below the equilibrium price creates a shortage (excess demand) where market forces automatically cause price to increase back to the equilibrium. Therefore, to be effective, a minimum price must be set above the equilibrium.

Student notes: Price controls – Minimum price

QUESTIONS & TASKS

1 Use the diagram below to answer the questions that follow.

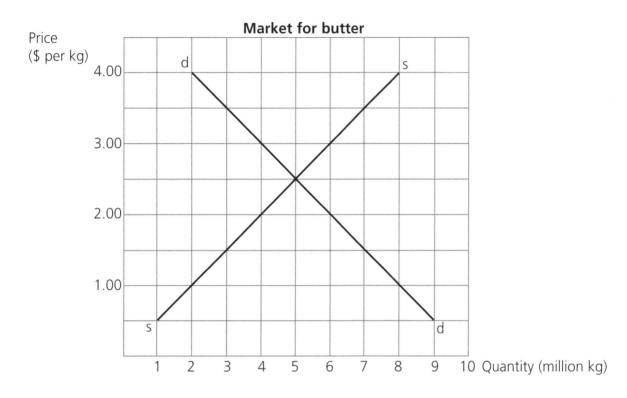

Market for butter

Price ($ per kg)

The government wants to protect producers from volatile prices in the world market for butter. One option is to impose a price control of $3.50 per kg.

a What is the correct economic term for this option?

_____

b Show the effect on the graph of the government imposing a price control of $3.50 per kg.

c What difficulty does the government face with getting a price control of $3.50 per kg?

_____

_____

_____

_____

d Why might a government impose a minimum price?

_____

_____

_____

Market for kiwifruit annually

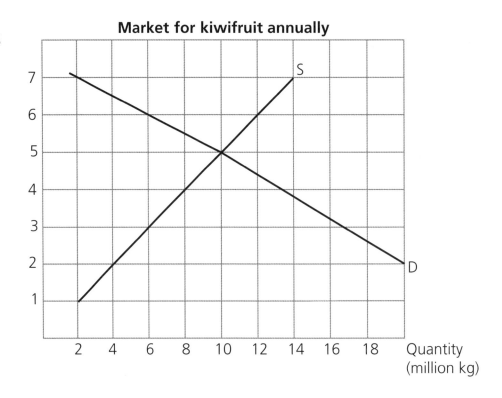

Price $ per kg

2 **a** Show a minimum price of kiwifruit set at $7 per kg.

b Referring to the graph above, identify and calculate:

	Before the minimum price	After the minimum price
Quantity sold		
Price consumers pay		
Consumer spending		
Price producers receive		
Producer revenue		
Change in the value of sales		
Change in producers' revenue		
Size of the surplus		

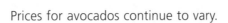

Prices for avocados continue to vary.

3 The graph shows the effects of a minimum price on the market for avocados.

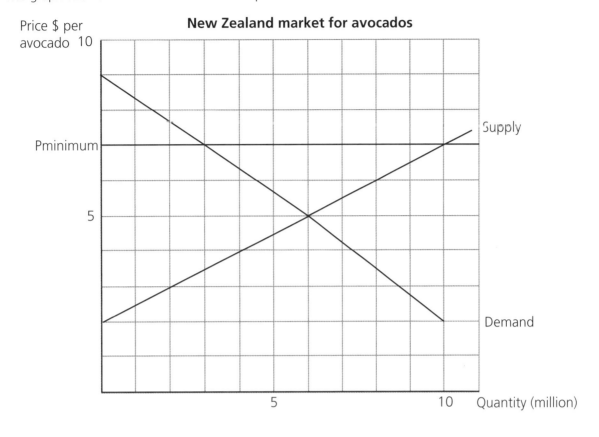

New Zealand market for avocados

Price $ per avocado

Pminimum

Supply

Demand

Quantity (million)

a On the graph above:

   (i) use dotted lines to show the original equilibrium price and quantity (label as **Pe** and **Qe**)

   (ii) use dotted lines to show the new quantity demanded (**Qd**) and supplied (**Qs**)

   (iii) label the resulting **surplus** or **shortage**.

b Fully explain the effects on consumers and producers because of the minimum price.

_____

_____

_____

_____

_____

_____

_____

_____

_____

_____

_____

_____

_____

_____

$\bigcirc$ Review (exam) questions

1 **a** On the graph of the Weekly market for organic eggs below, show the effect of a minimum price of $7 per dozen (labelled as Pmin).

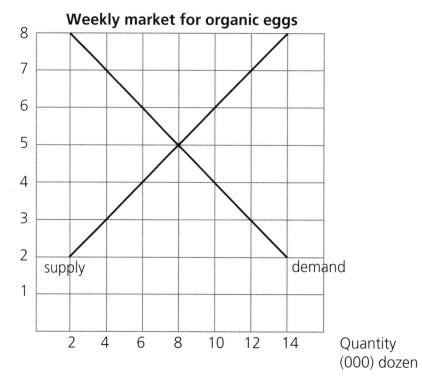

Price ($ per dozen)

Weekly market for organic eggs

Quantity (000) dozen

b Referring to the graph, identify:

• the price that consumers pay before and after the minimum price

before: _____ after: _____

• the price that producers receive before and after the minimum price

before: _____ after: _____

• the quantity that consumers buy before and after the minimum price

before: _____ after: _____

• the value of sales before and after the minimum price

before: _____

after: _____

• firms' income before and after the minimum price

before: _____

after: _____

c Fully explain the effects of introducing a minimum price for organic eggs on egg producers.
In your answer you should:

- explain the change in price
- explain the change in quantity demanded and quantity supplied
- explain the effect on organic egg producers
- refer to the data above.

Volatile prices for lambs is making the
government consider introducing a floor price.

2 a On the graph of the market for lambs below, show the effect of a minimum price of $150 per lamb
(label as Pmin). You must:
- show the equilibrium price (Pe) and quantity (Qe) before the minimum price
- show the new quantity demanded (Qd) and quantity supplied (Qs) after the minimum price
- label the resulting surplus or shortage.

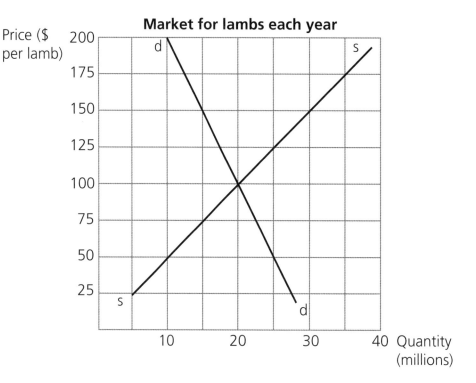

b Referring to the graph, identify:

- the price that consumers pay before and after the minimum price

  before: _____ after: _____

- the price that producers receive before and after the minimum price

  before: _____ after: _____

- the quantity that consumers buy before and after the minimum price

  before: _____ after: _____

c Fully explain the effects of introducing a minimum price for lamb producers.

In your answer you should:

- explain the change in price
- explain the change in quantity demanded
- explain the change in quantity supplied
- explain a flow-on effect for producers
- refer to the data above.

REVISION/STUDY
Tasks and activities

Exam hints

Preparation

Prepare for the exam by completing all exericises in this book, doing old papers or the written questions on eLearneconomics.com website.

In the exam

- Use appropriate economic language, examples and terms in your answers.

- Make accurate references in your answers to the resource material and/or graphs drawn, i.e., provide details in your descriptions, such as figures or names of individuals/firms/products.

- Take care and construct well-labelled, accurate graphs (with a title, graduated scales) using a ruler to plot curves. Refer to these graphs explicitly in your explanations, e.g., D1 to D2, P to P'.

- Write structured answers that link ideas, keep your answers on track and do not contradict what you have written.

- Read questions carefully and add reasons, causes and effects in your explanations.

- Flow-on effects need to be valid, explained in full and kept in context with the event that led to it, rather than a restatement of the initial event itself.

- Attempt all questions.

- Present answers in a legible form.

- Use a pen (not a pencil) on your script to ensure answers are clear.

- Do not use abbreviations or text language because these are not appropriate in a formal exam.

       ISBN: 9780170415972

Consumer choices using scarcity and/or demand

Terms & ideas

Ceteris paribus. _____
_____
_____

Change in demand. _____
_____
_____

Change in quantity demanded. _____
_____
_____

Choice. _____
_____

Complements. _____
_____
_____

Consumer. _____
_____

Consumer (or individual) demand. _____
_____
_____

Decrease in demand. _____
_____
_____
_____

Demand. _____
_____

Demand schedule. _____
_____
_____

Disposable income. _____
_____
_____
_____

Household. _____

_____

_____

Increase in demand. _____

_____

_____

_____

_____

_____

Inferior goods. _____

_____

_____

Law of demand. _____

_____

_____

Limited means. _____

_____

_____

Limited means – time. _____

_____

_____

_____

Limited means – money. _____

_____

_____

_____

_____

_____

Luxuries. _____

_____

_____

_____

_____

Needs (Necessities). _____

_____

_____

Opportunity cost. _____

_____

_____

Savings. _____

_____

_____

_____

Scarcity. _____

_____

_____

_____

Substitutes. _____

_____

_____

_____

Values. _____

_____

_____

_____

Wants. _____

_____

_____

Why consumers buy more at lower prices. _____

_____

_____

_____

_____

Question One: Consumer choice

Jackson works part time, either at the local cinema or pizza place. He spends the rest of his time making indie movies, going to the beach or reading. Jackson enjoys spending time with his friends and family.

a Refer to the resource material to explain how and why Jackson's choices result in an opportunity cost. Link the economic concepts of limited means, choice and opportunity cost in your answer.

_____

_____

_____

_____

_____

_____

_____

_____

_____

_____

_____

_____

_____

_____

_____

_____

_____

_____

_____

_____

_____

_____

_____

_____

_____

_____

_____

_____

_____

_____

_____

_____

_____

_____

_____

b Refer to the resource material on the previous page to explain how Jackson's values influence his decisions about how to use his time.

In your answer, include:

- what is meant by values
- an activity Jackson would choose to spend his time on if he valued financial security
- an activity Jackson would choose to spend his time on if he valued his friendships.

_____

_____

_____

_____

_____

_____

_____

_____

_____

_____

_____

_____

_____

_____

_____

_____

_____

_____

c Explain a possible compromise that Jackson could make to resolve any conflict between the two values.

_____

_____

_____

_____

_____

_____

_____

_____

_____

_____

_____

_____

_____

_____

_____

_____

_____

Question Two: Demand

Jackson catches up with his friends at the weekends, at the local cafés. His demand schedule for coffee is shown below.

Jackson's fortnightly demand schedule for coffee	
Price $	Quantity demanded (cups)
5	2
4	6
2	10
1	18

a Draw a fully labelled demand curve on the graph below using the information from the demand schedule above.

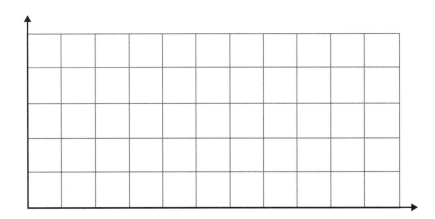

b (i) On the graph above, show the effect of the price of coffee decreasing from $4.00 to $2.00 per cup. Fully label your changes.

(ii) Explain the effect of the price decrease. Include a reason for the law of demand.

_____

_____

_____

_____

_____

_____

_____

_____

_____

_____

_____

_____

_____

Jackson sometimes has a slice of
ginger crunch with his coffee.

c Discuss how a decrease in the price of a cup of coffee will affect Jackson's demand for ginger
crunch. In your answer:
- explain the economic relationship between a cup of coffee and a slice of ginger crunch
- complete the graph below for ginger crunch
- refer to the changes in your graph.

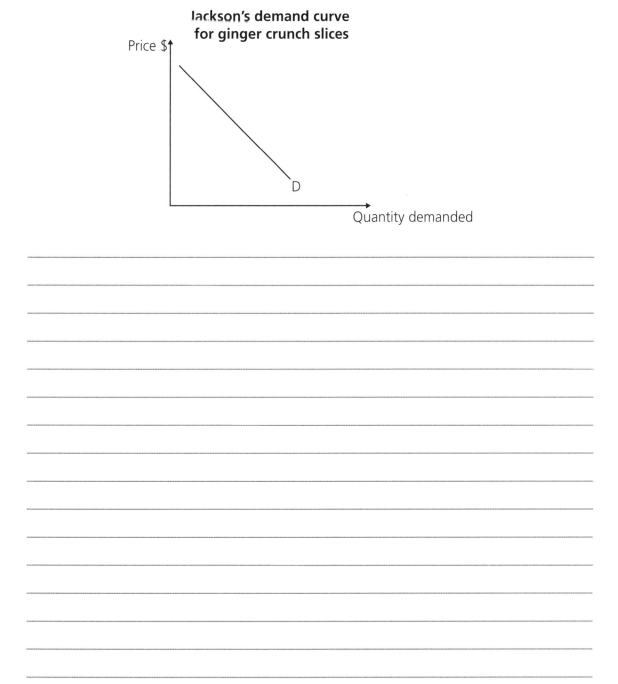

Jackson's demand curve
for ginger crunch slices

_____

_____

_____

_____

_____

_____

_____

_____

_____

_____

_____

_____

_____

_____

_____

_____

Question Three: Types of goods

Jackson will often grab dinner at the local food hall in the mall with friends, while at other times they will go out to an upmarket restaurant.

a Complete the sketch graphs below to show the effect an increase in direct tax rates would have on Jackson's demand for meals out.

Jackson's demand for restaurant meals

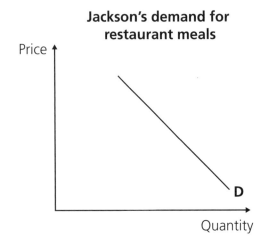

Jackson's demand for local food hall meals

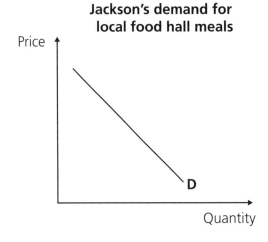

b (i) Explain the link between an increase in direct tax rates and disposable income.

(ii) Explain luxury goods and inferior goods in Jackson's context. Refer to your graphs.

(iii) Explain a possible flow-on effect this change may have for Jackson.

Producer choices, using supply

Terms & ideas

Change in quantity supplied. _____
_____
_____

Change in supply. _____
_____
_____
_____
_____

Costs of production. _____
_____
_____
_____

Decrease in quantity supplied. _____
_____
_____
_____
_____

Decrease in supply. _____
_____
_____

Environmental factor. _____
_____
_____

Flow-on effect. _____
_____
_____
_____
_____

Increase in quantity supplied. _____
_____
_____
_____

    ISBN: 9780170415972

Increase in supply. _____
_____
_____

Indirect tax. _____
_____
_____

Individual supply. _____
_____

Law of supply. _____
_____
_____

Legal factor. _____
_____
_____

Quota. _____
_____

Reasons for an increase in supply. _____
_____
_____

Related goods (products). _____
_____
_____
_____
_____

Subsidy. _____
_____

Supply schedule. _____
_____
_____

Technology/productivity. _____
_____
_____
_____
_____

Question One: Law of supply

a Complete the supply schedule using the graph provided.

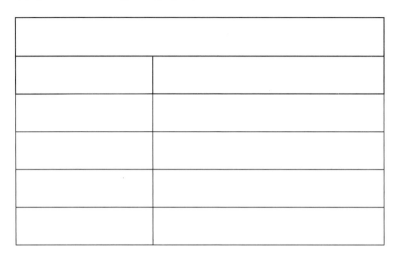

Tony's supply curve for smoked beef each week

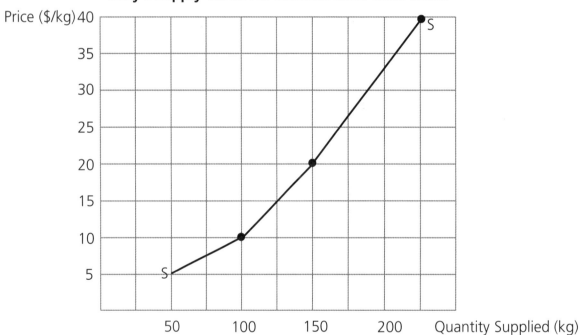

b On the graph above, show the effect on the quantity of smoked beef supplied if the price of smoked beef per kg decreases from $20 per kg to $10 per kg. Fully label all changes.

c • Define individual supply.
• Describe the law of supply by referring to the data from the price decrease.
• Explain the reason for the law of supply in the context of Tony's supply of smoked beef.
• Suggest a related good for smoked beef, and explain why it is a related good.
• Explain the impact of the change in price on Tony's supply of the suggested related good.

Question Two: Regulations

Tony produces his smoked beef products in his double garage from home. New local government bylaws that will ban commercial business manufacturing goods and services on domestic premises will affect his production.

a On the graph, show the effect of the ban on Tony's supply of smoked beef. Fully label your diagram.

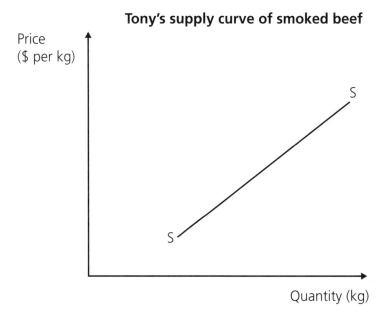

Tony's supply curve of smoked beef

Price
($ per kg)

S

S

Quantity (kg)

b Discuss the ban's impact on Tony's supply of smoked beef.

- Use an example to explain how the ban will affect Tony's smoked beef production.
- Refer to the changes on your graph.
- Explain a flow-on effect of this change.

_____

_____

_____

_____

_____

_____

_____

_____

_____

_____

_____

_____

_____

_____

_____

_____

_____

_____

_____

_____

_____

_____

_____

_____

_____

_____

_____

_____

_____

_____

Question Three: Technology

Recently Tony has purchased some new equipment that
will assist in the packaging of the smoked beef. This will
streamline his production process.

a On the graph, show how the new equipment is likely to impact on Tony's supply of smoked beef.

Tony's supply curve of smoked beef

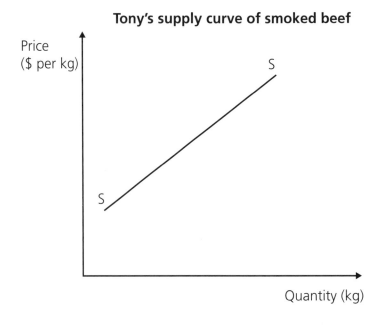

b Discuss the effect that the new equipment is likely to have on Tony's supply of smoked beef.

- Define productivity and technology and explain the link between these terms.
- Explain several flow-on effects for Tony of this change in the supply of smoked beef.
- Refer to the changes on your graph.

_____

_____

_____

_____

_____

_____

_____

_____

_____

_____

_____

_____

_____

_____

_____

_____

_____

_____

_____

_____

_____

_____

_____

_____

_____

_____

_____

_____

_____

_____

_____

_____

_____

Consumer, producer and/or government choices, using market equilibrium

Terms & ideas

Black market. _____

_____

_____

Equilibrium. _____

_____

_____

Market. _____

_____

_____

Market demand. _____

_____

Market supply. _____

_____

_____

Maximum price control (ceiling price). _____

_____

_____

Minimum price control (floor price). _____

_____

_____

Price controls. _____

_____

_____

_____

Shortage (excess demand). _____

_____

_____

_____

Surplus (excess supply). _____

_____

_____

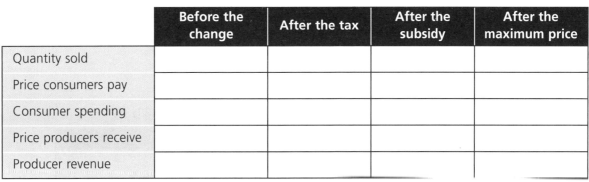

	Before the change	After the tax	After the subsidy	After the maximum price
Quantity sold				
Price consumers pay				
Consumer spending				
Price producers receive				
Producer revenue				

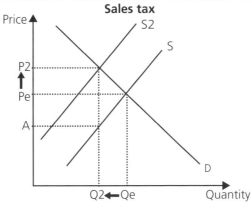

Government revenue from the tax: _____

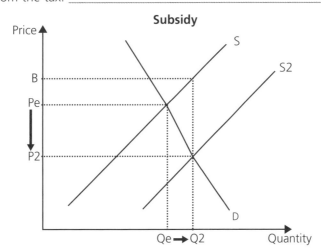

Cost to government of the subsidy: _____

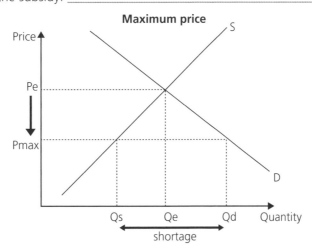

Size of the shortage: _____

Question One: Market equilibrium

a Use the information below to:

- complete the market supply table
- complete the market supply curve
- on the graph, identify the equilibrium price (**Pe**) and equilibrium quantity (**Qe**).

Market supply for wine in New Zealand (yearly)			
Price $ per bottle	North Island (million bottles)	South Island (million bottles)	Market supply (million bottles)
4	2.5	7.5	
8		22.5	30
16	11		40
20	15		50

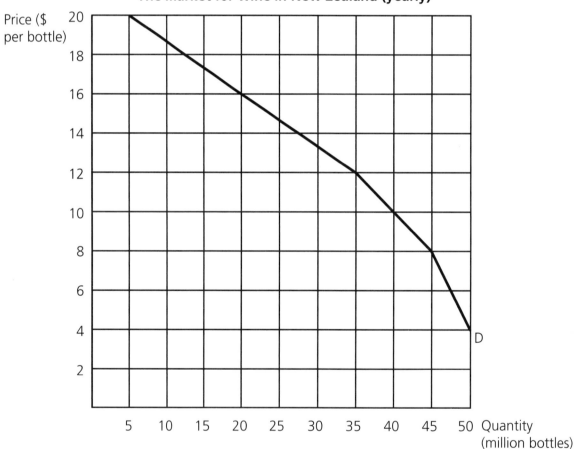

The market for wine in New Zealand (yearly)

Price ($ per bottle) / Quantity (million bottles)

D

b On the graph above, show the market situation of the price of a bottle of wine was $16 per bottle (**P2**). Use dotted lines to show the quantity supplied (**Qs**) and label the resulting **shortage** or **surplus**.

ISBN: 9780170415972

c Using your graph, explain how the market would react to the situation at $16 per bottle of wine. Use the terms quantity demanded, quantity supplied and shortage or surplus.

_____

_____

_____

_____

_____

_____

_____

_____

_____

_____

_____

_____

_____

_____

_____

_____

_____

_____

_____

_____

_____

_____

_____

_____

_____

_____

_____

_____

_____

_____

Question Two: Change in supply

In recent years, there has been a shift to planting grapes in areas that once had other crops.

a On the graph, label the new equilibrium price (**P2**) and equilibrium quantity (**Q2**). Label any resulting shortage/surplus at the original equilibrium.

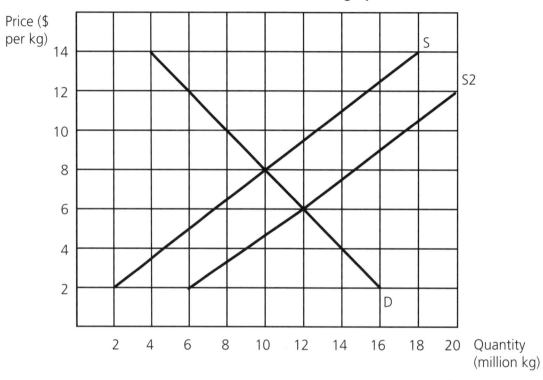

The New Zealand market for grapes

b Use the graph to complete the table.

	Before the change	After the change
Quantity sold		
Equilibrium price		
Producer revenue		

c Use the graph and explain the impact on the market. You must:
- explain how market supply is determined
- explain the change in price
- explain the effect of the change on quantity demanded
- explain the impact of the change on producers' revenue and a flow-on effect.

Question Three: Change in demand

Red wine sales increase as health benefits
are published in several medical journals.

Explain how a shift of the demand curve impacts on the market. In your answer:

- Explain how market demand is derived.
- Label the original equilibrium price **Pe** and equilibrium quantity **Qe**.
- Shift the demand curve to create a shortage. Label the new price **P2** and label the shortage created at the original price.
- Explain how the market will react.
- Explain how the change in demand will affect the revenue and profit of red wine producers.

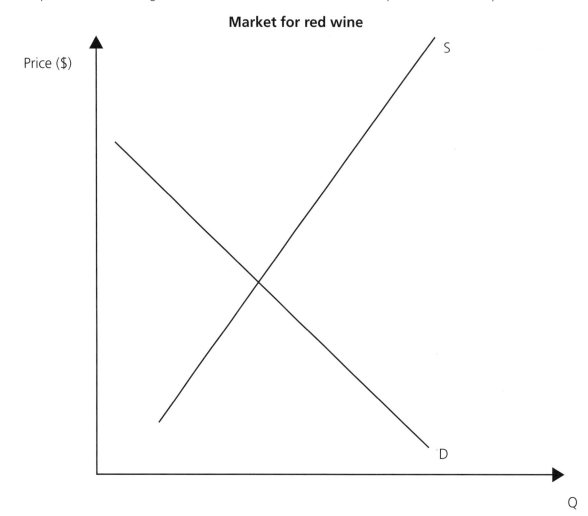

Market for red wine

Question Four: Indirect tax

Market for white wine yearly

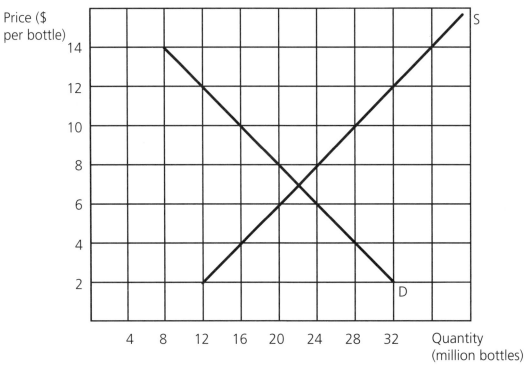

a On the graph above, show the effect of a $4 per unit sales tax. You must:
- use dotted lines and label the original equilibrium price (**Pe**) and equilibrium quantity (**Qe**)
- use dotted lines and label the new equilibrium price (**P1**) and new quantity (**Q1**).

b Refer to the graph, identify and calculate:

	Before the tax	After the tax
Quantity sold		
Price consumers pay		
Consumer spending		
Price producers receive		
Producer revenue		
Government revenue from the tax		

c Explain how the $4 per unit sales tax might affect different sectors of the economy.
   • Refer to the graph and your calculation.
   • Explain the change in price to consumers and consumer spending.
   • Explain the change in price to producers and producers' revenue.
   • Explain the effect on government and explain a possible long-term benefit to government.

_____
_____
_____
_____
_____
_____
_____
_____
_____
_____
_____
_____
_____
_____
_____
_____
_____
_____
_____
_____
_____
_____
_____
_____
_____
_____
_____
_____
_____

ISBN: 9780170415972

ISBN: 9780170415972